TRUE WISDOM

𝔑ihil 𝔒bstat.

RICARDUS A. O'GORMAN, O.S.A.,
Censor Deputatus.

𝔍mprimatur.

✠ FRANCISCUS,
Archiep. Westmonast.

DIE 14 SEPT., 1904.

VERA SAPIENTIA

TRUE WISDOM

Translated from the Latin of Thomas à Kempis

RIGHT REV. MGR. BYRNE, D.D., V.G.

(ADELAIDE, SOUTH AUSTRALIA)

R. & T. WASHBOURNE
1, 2 & 4 PATERNOSTER ROW, LONDON
BENZIGER BROS.: NEW YORK, CINCINNATI, AND CH CAGO
1904

ISBN: 0-9706526-7-4

Printed and Bound in the United States of America.

Published by:
St Athanasius Press
133 Slazing Rd
Potosi, WI 53820
1-800-230-1025
http://www.stathanasiuspress.com

Distributed by:
Mel Waller
St Joan of Arc Books
133 Slazing Rd
Potosi, WI 53820
1-800-230-1025
Wallmell@aol.com
http://www.stjoanofarcbooks.com
Our online bookstore specializing in pre-1964
used and new Catholic books or reprints thereof.

Check out our other titles on last page of book!

PREFACE

THE works of Thomas à Kempis need no praise, for they have stood the test of time, which commits to oblivion many works that had been once praised and widely read.

I have never seen an English translation of the work of Thomas à Kempis entitled ' Vera Sapientia ' (True Wisdom). A Latin copy of this work, published in Paris in 1804, came into my hands. Having read it with pleasure and profit, I did it into English. Friends to whom I showed it advised me to have it published, in the belief and hope that it would do good.

It was, moreover, suggested to have it published in London, from which it would have a larger circulation. It is well known that the language into which a work is faithfully translated suffers in purity and idiom. May I ask the reader to bear in mind this fact, and to excuse any defects which may be noticeable in this translation.

FREDERICK BYRNE.

CONTENTS

BOOK I

THAT VIRTUE HAS TO CARRY ON WAR WITH VICE

BOOK II

WHAT THINGS CAN BE TRULY AND JUSTLY CALLED GOOD AND BAD

BOOK III

THE MISERIES WHICH THE GOOD ENDURE IN THIS WORLD

BOOK IV

ON THE VIRTUES OF A TRULY CHRISTIAN MAN

TRUE WISDOM

BOOK I

THAT VIRTUE HAS TO CARRY ON WAR WITH VICE

CHAPTER I

THREE DIFFERENT MODES OF HUMAN LIFE

'I am the flower of the field and the lily of the valleys.'—
CANT. ii.

1. THIS is the voice of Christ to every devout soul.
For Christ is the beautiful Spouse of holy Church,
the head of all the faithful, the flower of all
virtues, the lily of the valleys, and the lover of
humility and chastity.

2. Whoever, therefore, wishes to serve Christ,
and to please the heavenly Spouse, should endeavour to overcome his vices, to gather the lilies
of virtues, to avoid idleness, to be employed in
what is useful, to pray often, to withdraw from
disputes, to love to be alone, to be silent of things
that do not concern him, or which perhaps are
even hurtful to him.

3. Exterior appearance, without interior virtue,

avails little before God. Attend, therefore, to your state of life, for you shall reap the reward of what good you will do, just as you shall bear the punishment of whatever evil you will have committed before God.

4. When, therefore, you eat or drink, sleep or rest, or go of your own desire where you will, you perform the works of the flesh, and become like the beasts, that roam about, eat, drink, and fill themselves till they are satisfied ; but when you watch and pray, sing psalms or hymns to God, or to His saints, or when you fast, and put away vice from you—when you do good to your neighbour, or when you are sorry, grieve, and weep for your sins, confess and implore pardon, you do then the works of the Holy Ghost, live according to the Spirit, and follow the rule of religious life ; you become like the holy angels in heaven, who praise God, publish His glory, bless His name, and always enjoy His presence.

5. But when you are proud or angry, detract or murmur, cheat, lie, or annoy others, rejoice at the losses that befall them, or are sad at their prosperity, when you deceive your neighbour and seek yourself in everything, you follow then the devil, and become like the evil spirits ; for they follow their passions and wickedness as much as they can, and to the extent they are permitted.

6. Therefore the life of the just is like that of the angels, the life of the carnal is equal to that of the beasts, and the life of the proud may be

compared to that of the devils. Beware, servant of God, lest you be entangled in their snares, be accused by them on the day of judgment, and put to shame.

CHAPTER II

THE SEVERE JUDGMENT OF GOD

'Let my heart rejoice, that it may fear Thy name.'—Ps. lxxxv.

1. My God, Thou art most lovable, but Thou art also most terrible. He who loves can rejoice, he who loves not should fear, but he who neither loves nor fears is foolish and insane. It is indeed a dreadful thing to fall into Thy hands. Who knows the power of Thy anger ? who can measure Thy wrath ? who can behold Thee in judgment ? who therefore should not fear Thee ?

2. There is no place where man is hidden from Thy face, for all things are uncovered and open to Thee ; Thou penetratest into the interior of man, and seest the most secret motions of his thoughts ; there is therefore no secret hidden from Thy eyes.

3. How terrible Thou art to sinners and to those hardened of heart, who are glad when they have done evil, and rejoice in most wicked things ; who say, The Lord does not see, and God does not understand ! They boast with vain words, as if Thou art not to come, and they turn away their face, that they may not see the end. But Thou

wilt come at an hour in which they do not think, and they shall be taken in the snares of their sins. For as thieves and robbers when caught are confused, so shall they be put to shame in due time. Thou wilt mock them who now despise Thy commands, and repay the wickedness of those who now hate justice.

4. Now they are deaf to Thy voice, but the time will come when they shall cry out, and nobody will hear them. They now turn Thy words into jests, but then they shall be turned into fire. For Thy word shall go forth with a terrible sound, and it shall strike the impious and wicked without mercy.

5. What will the proud puffed up with learning, and the great lifted up with power, then say ? What will they answer when the last trumpet will sound, and when Thou, O Lord our God, wilt appear in majesty with Thy angels and saints ? Then indeed shall be silent all the wicked and the scoffers of Thy word; they who did not fear Thee, and who persecuted Thy elect shall be slaughtered on every side.

6. They shall then be covered with great confusion, who, having put aside conscience and virtue, gave themselves up to vanity and lies. Everything that was then done through inordinate joy shall be turned into grief; companions in intemperance shall then be bound like fagots to be burned, and those whom love led into sin the avenging flame shall surround and torture.

7. Foolish and miserable, mad and blind lovers of the world, what do you, or what do you pretend ?   How shall you escape the anger of God ? Why do you hasten to eternal torments for a little pleasure which you love ?   Why have you not a dread of hell, who fear so much a little penance ? And you, who use every means to avoid the death of the body, why do you not do something to escape the death of the soul ?   Unless, therefore, you be converted, and do penance, you shall not escape the dreadful and fiery torments inflicted by an offended and just God.

8. I tremble when I consider that last day and hour, for God will not then be moved by prayers, but will be a just Judge to all.   O Holy God, Holy and Mighty, Holy and Merciful Saviour, do not deliver me to an evil death, but give me time to repent, that I may be able to weep sincerely for my sins before I depart from this life.

CHAPTER III

THAT WE SHOULD BE SORRY AND WEEP FOR OUR SINS

'My sorrow is always in my sight.'—Ps. xlvii.

1. My God, I have dishonoured my life by many sins, but behold the tears which in Thy presence I shed for them.   I know goodness does not abide in me, and whilst I live I shall not be free from sin.

2. Therefore I do wrong, and sin every day, and, what is worse, I allow many things to pass without true grief or sorrow ; for, in consequence of being occupied and entangled with external affairs and vain curiosities, I cannot quickly return to profitable sorrow. My sins very much increase in me darkness, by hindering the sources of grace and by preventing the rays of Divine consolation. Is this a small thing and trifling evil ? My God, it is a great evil, and becomes more dangerous, because it quickly passes from my heart, and does not cause in me any sorrow.

3. Dost Thou consider, O Lord, how often I trifle with Thee, and deceive myself ? Hast Thou, O Lord, been silent till now ? Where is the rod ? where is the lash ? where is the goad ? Why didst Thou withdraw Thy judgment and punishment from my sight ? If they had been present, thinkest Thou I would have acted so carelessly ? If Thou art silent for sake of my amendment, Thou manifestest Thy patience, but if I be negligent wilt Thou not punish me severely —if not here, certainly hereafter ? No sin, small or great, shall pass unpunished ; but it is much better to suffer here, where weeping is more profitable, labour shorter, satisfaction more acceptable, and reconciliation easier.

4. Do not therefore spare the rod, but fill my eyes with bitter tears, and do not put off my punishment to a future time, lest I be delivered to the torturers till I shall have paid the last

farthing ; for it is better to be lightly and mercifully punished now than to endure hereafter the
intense pains of purgatory.

5. I should therefore weep and have very great
sorrow for my sins.   I have no reason to laugh,
but many to weep ; darkness of mind, a slippery
conscience, falls into sin, and loss of grace, often
urge and force me to weep from very anguish of
heart.

6. What reason is there for mirth, considering
the divers temptations and assaults of the wicked ?
Spare me, O Lord—spare me !   Moved by sorrow
of heart, it is no wonder I weep, for the present
is the time of weeping.   Happy hour in which
arises in me sorrow for sin ; blessed tears which
flow from intensity of contrition produced by the
many stains of my soul.

7. Who is able to dispel completely this abyss
of darkness ?   Thou, my God, the true light,
canst dispel all the darkness of my soul ; Thou
canst give a new heart, create a clean heart, prepare a hidden tabernacle to be the place of Thy
abode, the tabernacle of Thy name ; for Thou
art the lover of purity, and the friend of a good
conscience.

8. But as Thou dost not willingly visit an
empty house—yea, Thou dost often abandon it
when it is the place of unruly passions—I am
therefore solicitous lest this should happen to me ;
but, most merciful and clement Lord, help me to
repair the injuries which sin has done in me.   Woe

to him from whom Thou departest in anger, but peace to him to whom Thou comest, and with whom Thou remainest.

9. Poor creature, placed in the midst of snares, and fettered with the chains of sin, what counsel can I follow, or what means of salvation can I have, but to lift up my sorrowful eyes to Thee, that Thou mayest hear my prayers from on high ? A burdened conscience cannot find or have a safer remedy than to offer itself contritely to Thee in prayer.   And how can troublesome temptations be better watched, lest they prevail, than by constant prayer poured forth to Thee, and by humbling myself exceedingly in Thy sight ?   But who will give me these good things, to pray and weep as I should ?   Whence shall I obtain this profound humility and abundance of tears ? From Thee, O Lord, with whom there is mercy and plentiful redemption.

10. O Lord God, the giver of every grace, grant that I may fittingly weep for even my smallest sins, for those which I have forgotten as well as for those of which I am conscious, and that I may do penance for all without exception.   May my sorrow and penance be acceptable to Thee ; may they restore to me the grace which I had lost, and may they procure for me greater and more efficacious means of salvation.

CHAPTER IV

LAMENTATION OVER TIME AND NEGLIGENCE

'Thy eyes did see my imperfect being.'—Ps. cxxxviii.

1. WHAT shall become of me, as I daily fall away? How shall I perfectly amend my life? When shall I become better? When shall I grow strong? and when shall I overcome the hindrances to my salvation? I am very much dispirited. Dost Thou think there is any hope for me to arise from sin, to amend my life, to advance in virtue, and to persevere to the end?

2. I have no trust in myself, and oh that my hope in Thee were firmer! I feel strong suggestions to despair, because my weakness is increased by continual trials, and I do not see an end of my grief and misery. And if I say I will now begin, now is the time, I will now strive to do my best, temptation is immediately present, the enemy arises against me, and my bad habits, in opposition to my will, firmly hold me. Behold, O Lord, my dejection, my misery, and the calamities which I suffer. Let Thy right hand be lifted up, and deliver me from those who oppress me, because their fear has fallen upon me, counsel has left me, my strength has faded away, my arm is broken, and my sword is unable to save me.

3. I do not see to whom to turn, and he who

would receive and comfort me does not appear. Thou alone hast continued to be my refuge, but because I have offended Thee I am afraid. I have sinned ; pardon me. I am very sorry for all my faults ; give me what Thou thinkest fit, and be propitious to me. Thou dost justly depart from me, and deliver me to the adversary. Remember, I beseech Thee, Thy creature who has fallen ; lift him up, for he cannot stand of himself. Attend to my cry and to my wants, be not forgetful of my labour and grief. Look, O merciful Father, on my banishment, captivity, imprisonment, and oppression, and deliver me who am in fetters from this prison of miserable slavery.

4. If a man shall have lived many years, shall he be the better of it ? Who knows whether he shall be better or worse ? The course and end of man is uncertain, and his perseverance doubtful, on account of the dangers of temptation and of his many falls into sin.

5. Many in the beginning of their conversion are humble and good, but afterwards they fall away and become rebellious ; at first they are fearful, devout, full of compunction, and silent ; afterwards they become free, dissolute, talkative, and unguarded. In the beginning they restrained their thoughts, afterwards they had scarcely any guard over their words and actions ; and so by little and little they fell deeply into sin by want of watchfulness in the beginning.

6. Who therefore should not fear and be cir-

cumspect, when it has sometimes happened that the good and modest fall into many misfortunes ? For who knows if he be chosen and able to bear all things ?   It is necessary that all shall be proved, and who is certain that he may not be burned, for fire is the trial ?   All should therefore fear, and should also hope for the best ; but they should not rashly presume or become careless by vain hope.

7. O Lord God, what joy can I have in the world when I begin to realize the uncertainty and weakness of everything under heaven ?   I am, however, certain of Thee, for Thou art good, and Thy mercy is from generation to generation to those who fear Thee.   Thy goodness and pity are infinitely greater than all my iniquities, and this will be my comfort so long as Thou givest me time to amend.

CHAPTER V

THE PRAYER OF A HUMBLE AND CONTRITE SPIRIT

' To Thee, O Lord, have I lifted up my soul.'—Ps. xxiv.

1. O LORD GOD, who wisely and justly disposest all things with angels and men and all creatures, accept, as great praises and thanksgivings due and now offered to Thee, all the tribulations and anguishes of my heart in sincere contrition for my sins.   Change for me every evil into good, and every good into what is always better, for

the glory of Thy name, and for the eternal salvation of my soul.

2. Thou knowest my weakness, my great ignor-
ance, and my inconstancy, by which I quickly
wander hither and thither far away from Thee.
Spare me, O Lord, according to the multitude of
Thy mercies, and quickly lead me back to Thee.
I desire to please Thy most benign countenance
with sacred gifts and prayers, especially with the
offerings of the poor, sorrow of heart, confession
of mouth, and satisfaction by good works.

3. I beseech Thee, my dearest Lord, to accept
my humble prayer and bitter sorrow for my sins,
for the sweet canticles of the angels and the united
prayers of all the heavenly citizens. I do not
despair, nor will I despair, of Thy pardon and
mercy, though I often fall and am oppressed by
my infirmity. I cease not, nor will cease, during
my life, from praising Thee ; I will glorify and
magnify Thee, O my God, till my soul is admitted
to Thy presence, for it is the greatest happiness
of the angels and blessed in heaven to always
praise and love Thee.

CHAPTER VI

COMPUNCTION OF HEART, OR THE GRIEFS AND
SIGHS OF A PENITENT SOUL

1. WEEP with me, all my friends ; see my sorrow,
for it is very great ; behold my wound, for it is
very deep. Why do I weep ? It is because I am

cast away from the face of God, and from the sight of His eyes. I sit in darkness and in the shadow of death ; I do not see the light of heaven.

2. Therefore what joy can I have—I, a miserable man, who went down from Jerusalem to Jericho, and fell into the hands of cruel robbers, who stripped me of the garment of immortality, and left me half dead from wounds inflicted on me ? The keepers that go about the city found me ; they struck and wounded me ; the keepers of the walls took away my veil.

3. Now, therefore, daughters of Jerusalem, tell the Beloved that I am filled with grief ; send messengers to Him, saying, ' Lazarus, whom Thou lovest, is sick '; ' Lord, my servant lieth at home sick of the palsy, and is grievously tormented.'

4. I am a son of Adam the prevaricator—a son of death, and born in sin. My entrance into the world was miserable, and my departure from it shall be fearful. Whither shall I flee ? I know not. If I ascend to heaven, Thou art there, and wilt not spare sinners ; if I descend into hell, Thou art there to punish the wicked.

5. Where shall I hide myself from the face of Thy anger, for I have sinned very grievously in my life ? I looked up to heaven, and God said, ' Take away the impious, that he may not see the glory of God.' I looked again into the abyss, and the terrible voice sounded in my ears, ' Bind his hands and feet, and cast him into exterior dark-

ness, where shall be weeping and gnashing of teeth.'

6. Fear and trembling came upon me, and darkness covered me from the face of the anger and indignation of the Lord.   And I said, Who therefore can be saved ?   If Thou, O Lord, wilt mark iniquity, who shall stand it ?   Terrible and holy is His name.

7. But now I have heard a consoling voice speaking to those who are in sadness and grief, saying, ' Blessed are they that mourn, for they shall be comforted '; and again, ' Do penance, for the kingdom of heaven is at hand '—the voice of the Lord consoling His servants, the voice of the Lord calling after them, ' Be converted and live, ye sons of men ; turn to Me, and I will turn to you.'   ' Come to Me all you who labour and are burdened, and I will refresh you.'

8. Now, my soul, do not fear so much.   ' The Son of man came to seek and to save that which was lost ;' and again, ' I have not come to call the just, but sinners.'   Therefore, my soul, animate thyself with great confidence, for the Lord has spoken. Thy life was drawing near to hell, and thou wert delivered to death, but God had mercy on thee, and resolved to show thee mercy.

9. Thou didst very much fear the face of the Lord, and didst think of hiding thyself from Him, as thy father Adam did when he sinned ; but this was a vain thought.   Thou didst also think of flight into a distant country, as did Jonas by

ship from the face of the Lord ; but in this thou didst act foolishly, for neither by hiding nor by fleeing canst thou escape the hand of the Lord. Return therefore to the heavenly kingdom by another way which God will point out to thee, that thou mayest walk therein.

10. This is the way : do penance. The best counsel and greatest help will be given thee from heaven. The counsel is that thou sincerely repent, and by weeping make reparation for thy sins, and thus reconciled thou shalt have peace with God. The help will be from the Lord, who made heaven and earth, and who, great as He is, deigned to pay all thy debts ; for He delivered His soul unto death, and prayed for transgressors that they should not perish, and by His death He rescued thee from eternal death, and saved thee by His cross.

11. The Apostle St. Paul reminded the faithful of this, saying, ' He bore our sins, fixing them to the cross, forgiving our offences that we might live with Him.' Hence in another place the same Apostle says, 'A faithful saying and worthy of all acceptation, that Jesus Christ came into the world to save sinners.' Behold the consolation and great hope God has given to sinners, and to the penitent and converted. Remember Thy holy word, by which Thou hast given me hope ; and, O Lord, I now prostrate myself before Thee in prayer, and cry to Thee from the bottom of my heart.

CHAPTER VII

THE DEVOUT PRAYER OF A SINNER TURNING TO GOD, AND IMPLORING MERCY

1. LORD GOD, Holy Father, I have sinned against heaven and before Thee, and am not worthy to be called Thy son, but, my Father, make me as one of Thy servants. If Thou dost cast me from Thy face, Thou dost justly, but Thou wilt act mercifully by receiving me, unworthy of every kindness.

2. Confiding in Thy mercy, I cast myself at Thy feet, and devoutly kiss them, shedding tears. I adore and supplicate Thee from a humble and contrite heart. Look, O merciful God, upon an insect and dead dog, and be propitious to me, as Thou wert to the holy Mary Magdalen, once a sinner, but who quickly obtained pardon at Thy feet.

3. Show forth Thy mercy to those who know Thee, extend Thy right hand to Thy fugitive servant, that Thy most pure eyes may see the contrition of my heart. Let not my Lord be angry for ever on account of the wickedness of His servant, but remember the great multitude of Thy mercies from the beginning, and be now appeased with Thy servant. Hear. O Lord, this one petition, which Thy servant on bended knees sends forth before Thy omnipotence, whilst he adores on earth the countenance of Thy glory.

I acted foolishly and very unwisely in so often offending Thy meekness, and in not fearing Thy majesty. Forgive, I beseech Thee, every offence of Thy servant, and do not blot out my name from the book of the living, but deign to write it in the number of Thy elect, that I may praise and glorify Thy holy name. Amen.

4. How great is Thy mercy, O Lord, who didst free from death man, deserving of death, in order to show forth more abundantly Thy goodness· Moreover, thou didst endeavour to call back those who had departed, and those who were going from Thee, by sending Thy faithful servants and friends at the hour of supper to say to the invited that all things are ready, and to come to the marriage. Thou couldst, in the order of justice, have sent armies after Thy enemies, who refused that Thou shouldst reign over them, to kill those murderers, who deserved to be either thrown into prison till they paid the last farthing, or to be cast away with those who are in hell. Thou didst not exercise Thy power, but showed Thy usual meekness by bearing patiently all things for the time, that Thy chosen ones might be free, and flee from the face of Thy wrath—that is, might prevent by sincere repentance Thy terrible judgment.

5. For if Thou didst put forth Thy hand against the wicked, and all those who sinned, Thou shouldst have lost many who have now become Thy friends, and found a place with Thee among Thy great saints. Thou shouldst not now have

2

Peter, who sinned by denying Thee three times ; nor Paul, who by persecuting the Church blasphemed Thee ; nor Matthew the publican, who was intent on acquiring riches ; not even Thy principal and great Apostles, whom Thou hast made judges over all the earth. Thy omnipotent hand and Thy mercy did this, and Thy right hand is full of all goodness.

6. For, hiding all Thy anger, Thou desirest to make us sons of grace, partakers of Divine nature, and coheirs of Thy kingdom. O fountain of piety and infinite mercy, which never ceases to flow abundantly, and continues always to reach those that approach Thee, oh that all would draw near to Thee, and taste of the delicacies of Thy table ; for they are sweet, have no bitterness or germ of death. But Thou art not well pleased with all, for many turn backwards, loving this world more than the company of Thy holy sons, giving up all hope, and serving uncleanness and wickedness, to whom remains certain judgment. Separated far from Thee, they consider those things pleasures under which are thorns.

7. But Thy beloved sons and faithful servants hate sin and love Thee with their whole hearts, meditate night and day on Thy commandments ; and these Thou protectest under Thy wings, lest they should be entangled by the snares of the world. These often burn with an ardent desire of eternal life, and wish quickly to be dissolved, that they may more happily live with Thee.

8. And when they are not heard, the delay is caused by Thy will, and for their salvation, that they may be more exercised in labour. Not that Thou, O Lord, lovest them less, when Thou dost not immediately comply with their prayers and desires, but by delaying them Thou wishest to reward more abundantly those whom Thou permittest to be more afflicted in this world. It is well for those who have received from Thee so great a grace, who now burn with a desire of eternal life, and who by reason of their good works await a rich reward.

9. I who am a sinner, and weighed down with the burden of sins, how shall I dare to lift up my eyes to those high mountains, Thy saints and perfect men, who by the depth of their conversion soared above this earthly habitation, this valley of tears, and by the height of contemplation now reach heaven. Woe, woe, woe, says St. John the Apostle, to the inhabitants of the earth ; woe to carnal minds, that even by desire live in this world ; woe also to those who are surrounded by the incitements of many passions ; and woe also to those who stray far away from the path of the just, who weep not, but foolishly laugh, and, what is worse, when they do wrong in the presence of God, fear not, but even think nothing of it.

10. Lament now, ye sons of men ; weep for yourselves, ye children of Adam, who feed on ashes as bread, and who have changed heavenly food for earthly. Unhappy and blind children,

what have you lost ?　Because you do not know, you therefore do not weep, and you are the more to be mourned for because you do not see your misery.

11. Is it therefore wonderful that I grieve—if I truly grieve, as I should ?　For internal sorrow changes the affections of men ; it will neither allow him to rejoice nor to be comforted by worldly things.　Do not delay help to Thy unworthy servant, and do not allow him to continue longer after the vanities of the world.　I have wandered like a sheep that has gone astray ; look after Thy sheep, O Lord, for it is time.　It is not my justice or my goodness, O Lord, but Thy mercy and meekness, that are beyond all measure.　Do to me Thy servant according to Thy mercy, and visit me with Thy saving grace, that I may live in the goodness of Thy elect and be glad in the joy of Thy people, that Thou mayest be praised by Thy inheritance which Thou didst acquire with Thy blood ; who with the Father and the Holy Ghost art God blessed for ever.　Amen.

CHAPTER VIII

WATCHFULNESS AND PRAYER ARE TO BE EMPLOYED IN TEMPTATIONS

1. WATCH and pray, that you enter not into temptation, either of the flesh, the spirit, the devil, or the world.　The flesh suggests concupiscence,

the spirit pride, the devil envy, and the world vanity. Christ teaches the contrary : He exhorts us to practise chastity, humility, charity, and contempt for the world, in order to merit the kingdom of God and to escape the pains of hell.

2. You should therefore watch and pray, at all times and in every place, because nowhere is there safety from the envious enemy, who sleeps not, and ceases not from tempting, but goes about and seeks whom he may deceive and trouble, whom he may hinder from holy exercises, and induce to give up prayer. Therefore our Lord Jesus Christ, knowing the wickedness of the devil, the usefulness of prayer, the strength of the enemy and the weakness of man, admonished His disciples and all the faithful to watch and pray, if they wish to overcome their enemies—that is, their vices.

3. Watch therefore and pray, that you enter not into temptation of the devil, and consent to him. If you cannot read the whole psalter, read one psalm or one verse, or one devout hymn to Jesus or Mary or some saint, in order to raise up your heart to God by a sigh or vocal prayer. For God is present to all calling on Him with humility, for the humble prayer of the just penetrates heaven, gives confidence with God, and sets at nought the wiles, the strength, the alarms, and deceits of the devil. If you are hindered in public by men, enter your chamber according to the

counsel of Christ, and, having closed the door, pray to the Father in secret ; for He knows what is in your mind, what you desire, and of what you have need.

CHAPTER IX

AN ENCOURAGEMENT TO SPIRITUAL ADVANCEMENT

1. SWEET indeed and agreeable to my ears are the words of the Apocalypse, which says, ' He who has ears, let him hear what the Spirit says to the Churches : I will give to him who overcomes a hidden manna.'   The proper meaning of which is, I will give spiritual consolation to him who despises carnal ; I will bestow heavenly and interior gifts, which of themselves excel all other pleasures, on him who despises worldly and exterior things. For so great are those spiritual gifts that no one is deserving of them till he first learns to despise vain and vile ones ; for it is written, ' The senseless man shall not know nor the fool understand these things.'

2. I will here speak more freely about resisting vice and overcoming bad habits. As the Lord formerly rained down manna for the children of Israel journeying through the desert, so also He now sends to His spiritual children the grace of interior consolation, to enable them to bear the trials of this world. As the children of Israel were nourished with this food till they reached

the land of promise, so the elect are nourished with the bread of life so long as they are pilgrims in this world, till, having cast off the body, they enter into the land of the living.

3. Why do you neglect your own advancement ? Your labours are certainly for yourselves and for your own peace. The Scripture says, ' I laboured little, and I have found great rest.' But perhaps you will answer, Who is able to fight always against vices and passions ? They appear to be numerous and almost insurmountable ; who is able to bear so great vexation ?

4. Hear, you incredulous and rebellious, you faint-hearted soldiers and idle servants. You look to the labour, you think of the warfare, but why do you not consider the victory and reward ? What is the labour to eternal rest ? what is the short struggle to the consolation of a good conscience ? Oh, if you would only begin, and bravely and resolutely propose to yourselves to either conquer or die, you should find, by the grace of God, that very light which now appears insurmountable. Seldom or never is anyone found so bad but that he can become virtuous by diligence and perseverance.

5. It appears to you hard to overcome your passions, but unless you bring them under subjection, you shall never have true peace of heart. For when others are with God in devotion and peace, you shall be sad, troubled, and unhappy, both within and without. Never shall you be at

rest and truly joyful, unless you mortify your carnal desires.

6. If the piety of the saints and the devotion of many do not influence you, let at least your own miseries and the sentence of Divine justice terrify you ; for it is said, ' I will heap evils upon them, and will spend my arrows among them ; they shall be consumed with famine, and birds shall devour them with a most bitter bite.' Oh that you would change your former life, so that, having become altered and fervent, the promises of the Holy Ghost would daily make you better and more courageous. The Lord says, ' I will give to him who overcomes a hidden manna ; if you incline to Me and hear Me, you shall eat of the goods of the earth.' The beautiful rose shall spring up instead of the thorn, and the candid lily instead of the weed. These are great things, sweet and consoling to those desirous of advancing in virtue.

7. Be not, therefore, O man of God, disturbed or dejected by the multitude of your passions. Believe in God and hope in Him, and you shall be a conqueror greater than you had been. The Lord will fight for you, and you shall be silent. Do you understand this ? The Lord Himself will give you strength to resist anger, to shake off sloth, to refuse consent to concupiscence ; and you shall be silent, because you do not attribute this power to yourself, you are not puffed up on

account of it, but you refer it entirely to God, who is at the right hand of the poor.

8. Also, as much,as you can, withdraw yourself from men, and confess that you are nothing but a weak and poor creature. If at any time an adversary will stand up and say what is displeasing to you, be patient and silent. What harm can the ill-will of another do you ? If he be angry with you, if he detract you, and if he reproach you, he rather shows that he himself is not virtuous. If you be good and patient he can do you no harm ; on the contrary, by the exercise of the virtue of patience your merit is increased, and you are more esteemed by the wise for having borne reproach.

9. A man will bear exterior trials as his interior is regulated, for if you are good, simple, upright, and fearing God, no one can take from you your goodness, justice, and peace, unless you yourself voluntarily lose them. Learn, at least, to be silent when injured, because in the time of trouble silence is great prudence. He who desires to conquer should overcome himself. Think of the reward, and not of the injury. How can you edify another if you will not bear anything disagreeable, but answer back in your zeal for good ? If he does not forgive, do you pardon, for it often happens that he who is angry with another is guilty of a greater sin than he who bears with anger. The miserable generally complain, and the impatient are often angry and blame others.

10. How justly and prudently you would act if you first exercised your zeal against your passions, and corrected in yourself what you reprehend in others. What does it profit me to correct others, and to continue in my own sins ? It is good for him who profits from my bad example, but woe to me who am the destroyer of my own salvation.

11. Be therefore ashamed that you have not yet learned to bear with the little failings of your brother, you who every day desire that your own faults be borne with by others. Why, therefore, do you not show that mercy to another which you would wish to be done to yourself ?

12. Beware, therefore, lest he who appears a sinner go before you into the kingdom of God, and you, presuming on your goodness, become like the proud Pharisee who was condemned by the Lord for his pride in opposition to the humility of the publican. You have now heard in some way, my beloved, how you should overcome yourself, and exercise zeal against your own failings.

13. Endeavour, therefore, always to lessen something of your bad habits, and to advance more and more in virtue. As negligence is conducive to foster bad habits and to lessen virtue, so diligence overcomes and roots out vices of long standing. Though you have to labour in the beginning of the warfare, yet, when you see your enemies gradually fall away, you shall have hope of a prosperous end.

14. The fear of doing violence to our nature is a very great hindrance to us. How many labours do men undergo to acquire temporal goods, and we become languid about eternal ones! The sailor ventures upon the stormy seas, the merchant travels through many lands, the soldier exposes his life in battle, the labourer toils from morning till night in delving the earth. Without labour riches are not acquired, honours are not obtained. Why, then, do we think that virtue can be obtained without labour ?

15. Do something to-day, add a little to-morrow, and so each day virtue is added to virtue, resolution to resolution, and this makes a man virtuous, devout, pure, holy, religious, dear to God and beloved by men. A man following this course overcomes vice, beautifies his interior, and often enjoys heavenly consolations which are unknown to the carnal and slothful. Let us, therefore, again and again turn over in our minds the text, ' I will give to him who overcomes a hidden manna.' It will encourage us to labour against sloth, to be zealous in pursuit of our spiritual advancement ; it will be a check to our vices, and will bring to us an increase of heavenly gifts. The Holy Ghost will not deprive His faithful soldiers of their reward, but whilst bravely fighting He will sound in their ears these encouraging words, ' To him who overcomes 1 will give a hidden manna.'

CHAPTER X

A DETERMINED FIGHT IS TO BE CARRIED ON AGAINST VICE, AFTER THE EXAMPLE OF THE SAINTS

'Do ye manfully, and let your heart be strengthened.'—
Ps. xxx.

1. As we learn to bear adversity from the passion and cross of Jesus, and from the sufferings of the holy martyrs, so we also learn to overcome carnal vices, to despise riches, to flee honours, to treat with contempt all worldly things, and to seek and love heavenly, after the example of the Blessed Virgin, of virgins, holy widows, and chaste servants of God. Study, O servant of God, to imitate the unconquerable patience of brave men, to reach the devil and his wiles, to despise and cast away from you all pleasures of the flesh, with all other vices.

2. If God in His goodness has given to you temporal goods, do not, miserable man, be puffed up with them. Do not foolishly set your heart on them, for you do not know how long you shall be here to enjoy them. Do not desire a long life, but a good one, for a good conscience is better than all the treasures of the world. The more you have of earthly goods, the more severely you shall be judged.

3. Oh the deceitful favour and short glory of

the world! How happy the men and prudent
the virgins who left all for Christ, and studied to
reach their eternal country by the narrow path.

4. Know, therefore, you faithful and devoted
servants of Jesus Christ, that so long as you live
it is necessary for you to watch and pray, to fast
and labour, and to fight against various carnal
and spiritual temptations. It is necessary to
chastise the flesh, and to repress its risings against
the spirit, in order that it may not deceive and
prevail against the soul, and lead it to hell. What
does it profit to nourish the flesh delicately here,
and afterwards to be grievously tortured in
hell ?

5. What advantage is it to be praised here and
honoured by men, and afterwards to be put to
shame and condemned with the wicked and
devils ? Those who are esteemed learned and
great in this world, but who are not found among
the elect, shall suffer confusion and shame before
God and His saints ; but to suffer and to be
despised for Christ by evil-doers is the greatest
honour, praise, and glory with God and His
saints.

6. Hence He gives consolation to His disciples,
and to all the faithful who suffer injuries and
oppressions for His name, saying, ' Blessed shall
you be when men shall hate you and reproach
you for My name. Be glad and rejoice, for your
reward is very great in heaven.'

CHAPTER XI

THAT CONSCIENCE IS TO BE GUARDED AT ALL TIMES AND IN EVERY PLACE

'My soul is always in my hands.'—Ps. cxviii.

1. There is nothing so useful or so salutary to one who desires to possess eternal life than to think always on the salvation of his soul. Read and examine everything, and you shall find that salvation cannot be found unless in God and in a good life. Hence the Lord and Redeemer of souls said to His disciples, ' What does it profit a man to gain the whole world and to lose his own soul ?'

2. He who thinks often of this has greater care of the salvation of his soul than of temporal gain or carnal pleasures. He is indeed a wise trader, who prefers and seeks eternal and spiritual goods before those that are passing.

3. Blessed is the servant who is faithful and prudent over a few things, who usefully employs his time, is silent about things that do not concern him, who is as one deaf and dumb for God's sake, passes peacefully through the troubles of the world, and has always his salvation before his eyes.

4. Do not, therefore, curiously inquire into the affairs of others, unless charity or compassion requires it. Do not desire the praises of men,

which are vain, or fear their reproaches, which
cannot harm you. They humble and purify
your soul, and merit for you a great crown in
heaven. No one is worthy to be elevated by
God but he who knows how to suffer reproaches
for Him. For as Thou, O Lord God, didst suffer
for me, so I should suffer for Thee, and follow
Thee to the best of my power, for Thou didst say
to St. Peter, ' Follow Me.'

5. I feel ashamed, O Lord, that I suffer so
little for Thee. I make many promises, but I
scarcely keep one out of ten. Many are my
words, but few my works. I am entirely in
fault and without excuse, for my sloth and
negligence increase my sins. What, therefore,
should I think or say but to ask pardon for
these things, and pray—I have sinned, O Lord ;
have mercy on me. All the saints have taught
and done this, and the faithful continue to do
the same. All ye saints and friends of God, pray
for me, who am weak and need every help, and
I humbly ask the assistance of all. O Holy of
Holies, O my Lord God, incline Thy ear to the
prayer of Thy poor servant ; help me, and I shall
be saved, and I will always meditate on Thy
justice. Oh that I could merit to be one of the
flock in Thy kingdom, which Thou hast prepared
for the humble and for those who love Thee. I
will therefore love Thee, O Lord, my strength,
with my whole heart, as Thou hast commanded
me. Thou art my entire hope, my salvation

and desire. Give me a clear understanding against every error, a clean heart against all impurity, a lively faith against every doubt, a firm hope against every distrust, fervent charity against all sloth and negligence, great patience against all tribulation, holy meditation against evil imaginations, continual prayer against the assaults of the devil, diligent attention to reading against the frequent wanderings of the mind, useful occupation against weariness and sleep, and devout remembrance of the Sacred Passion for the mortification of all vices. Help me with these graces, O my God, and comfort me with all Thy holy words. Amen.

CHAPTER XII

ON SOLITUDE AND SILENCE

'Lo, I have gone far off, fleeing away, and I abode in the wilderness.'—Ps. liv.

1. WHY? Because of the many benefits coming from it, and of avoiding the distractions of my heart, by hearing and seeing many things; for when the eyes do not see and the ears do not hear, the heart is not disturbed or grieved. To be hid and to be silent are conducive to peace of heart and to proficiency in devout prayer.

2. This is promoted in a retired place, far away from the crowd, where there is no noise. For a

a fish from the water soon dies, so a monk from his cell is quickly distracted and deteriorates. The prudent bee, collecting honey from flowers, immediately flies away, gladly seeks the hive, and carefully deposits it, that it may have food for winter ; and it conceals its sweet odour, that it may not lose its labour by wandering abroad. Precious spices closed in a case have a strong scent, but when opened and exposed quickly lose their strength. Roses grow in gardens safely fenced, but scattered upon the road they wither and are trampled underfoot.

3. A man often seen abroad, wandering and unsettled, is despised, but retired from the crowd and remaining at home is esteemed as a saint. Therefore love solitude and silence, if you wish to be devout and to possess internal peace. One needs to be very strong and guarded who mixes with men, and is not interiorly entangled with hurtful things.

4. Therefore remain willingly in solitude, that the evil spirit with all his phantoms may be far from you. A certain devout lover of silence said, ' Rarely do I speak long with men without some uneasiness of conscience.' And another said, ' A conversation should be very edifying to be better than silence '; a third said, ' A word said in its time is good '; and a fourth added, ' He who keeps his mouth firmly closed does not detract or lie.'

5. Oh, how praiseworthy and agreeable is the conversation in which there is no evil, no vanity,

no deceit, no lying! Many speak a great deal, but not without danger of the tongue prone to evil. He, therefore, who guards his mouth, remains in solitude, and prays often, has much peace. A certain youth asked an old religious, ' What rule in the Order is most conducive to peace and devotion ?' He answered in these remarkable words : ' To observe the silence prescribed by the Fathers, to shun the noise of men, and to avoid idleness.'

6. These three things are very necessary, and pleasing to God and His saints—that is, manual labour against idleness, love of study against weariness, and constant prayer against the deceits of the devil. The ancient, as well as the modern, holy Fathers have praised these things, because a silent man devoted to God is blessed by Him from above, and he is found better prepared and enlightened to contemplate Divine secrets. But the wanderers, and the talkative, who idly go about, render themselves unworthy of heavenly gifts, and are an annoyance to others.

7. The proud know not how to be silent for any time, because they wish to appear learned and to be praised above others. He who presumptuously speaks is censured by others, but he who is modestly silent obtains favour from the present. It is great humility of heart to think lowly of one's self and well of others.

8. It is great pride to abound in your own opinion, and to be obstinate in your own will, in

opposition to that of God and of the community of brethren. This is the worst leprosy, which God hates, and which He often punishes with a sudden death. The simple, innocent, humble, and obedient are always joyful and safe.

9. To be of few words, to avoid small faults, to say what is useful, and to do all things modestly, is praiseworthy. Let all things be done in order, for order is a most beautiful virtue. This is what Christ says, ' Have salt in you, and have peace among yourselves '; and St. Paul said, ' Let all your works be seasoned with salt.'

10. The chaste and virtuous man guards his heart, his mouth, and all his senses, which are always prone to evil, that he may not sin and offend God and his neighbour. He who willingly listens to vain things and narrates them to others has not compunction of heart.

11. He who does not guard the entrance to his heart and mouth shall very soon lose the graces of compunction ; for a man given to talking shall easily go beyond the propriety of conversation. If you had Jesus crucified fixed in your heart, a vain or idle word would not easily come from your lips ; but because you have not Jesus fixedly enclosed in your heart, you therefore seek from without vain and useless consolation, which gives little help to assuage the anguish of your heart.

12. Jesus alone gives true consolation to the soul, and heals all the wounds of vice ; for He is

able in an instant, and by one word, to deliver
the sorrowful from all evil, for the grace of God is
more powerful in good than sin is in evil. Why
do you listen to the vain rumours of the world,
which often disturb and distract the heart?
Why do you neglect the sweet words of Christ,
which can console and comfort you in every
temptation by night and by day?

CHAPTER XIII

HOW THE FAITHFUL MIND IS AFFECTED BY VARIOUS TEMPTATIONS BY WHICH IT IS ASSAILED OR TO WHICH IT IS NOW SUBJECT

1. As temptation is conducive to purify the interior man, to make him more virtuous, and to
give him a clearer perception of spiritual things,
it has therefore come upon me and begun to
exercise me.

2. Unless, therefore, the Lord had helped me
when I was so grievously oppressed that I thought
I could scarcely live—' unless the Lord had been
my helper, my soul had almost dwelt in hell.'
But He, who is accustomed to be present to the
troubled of heart, had pity on me; for who could
have borne with so many temptations, unless God
was my helper and protector?

3. But that I was able to stand against the
storm was His mercy, and that I yet stand

is the gift of His pity. Hence, whilst I live I will not trust myself, for though the sky appears calm, yet I will not conclude there will be safety, for the air becomes soon disturbed unexpectedly.

4. I have so much the more need of the protection of my Beloved, by so much the more I experience that every day brings its dangers. Nowhere is there safety but in heaven, where my Beloved feeds the elect with joy and gladness. But when will He place me in this place of pasture, where Satan is not and every evil is excluded ?

5. I have laboured up to the present on the sea, and I know not, on account of storms arising from every quarter, whether I shall reach the port of safety. Nothing, therefore, as regards myself is safe ; but I have for my shield and protection the resolution that I shall always be guided by the light of faith, that I shall humbly ask for the grace of my Beloved, that I shall always have the greatest hope in Him, that I shall never consent to be separated from His love, and finally that I shall commit myself to the abyss of His providence and mercy rather than to my own industry.

6. Therefore, though I may often waver and fall, yet I will never despair, but instantly pray and cry out to thee : Lord, my God, have mercy on my soul, and do not allow me to be endangered in temptations, but faithfully help me bravely to resist and overcome them. Extend Thy right

hand to Thy creature, whom Thou provest by Satan, and dost often place in trial.

7. If temptation so violent should assail and hinder me from calling out to Thee, I will send forth sighs from the bottom of my heart; for Thou knowest the hidden things of my heart, and what the Spirit desires. For it is not His will that one of His little ones who believes in Him should perish.

8. Oh, how great is His goodness to be with me in temptation, even when I am ignorant of it and do not advert to it.

9. He has very often saved me from being given over to my passions, but it sometimes happens, by His secret judgment, that I fall and am overcome in little things, lest I should be proud and presume in great things, and that I should learn to be humble and diffident; for I am nothing even when I seem to be firm and exalted.

10. I advise you, therefore, not to hastily or foolishly praise me, though I do fairly well, but to reserve your praise to the end of a holy life; rather, indeed, praise God, not me. May the great God alone be praised who so often assists me in temptation, and in pity deliverest me from their assaults, sometimes by sending forth His arrows against those coming in crowds to overcome me : 'He sent forth His arrows to scatter them, He multiplied His lightnings to terrify them.' After this I had a little rest, by reason of my Beloved giving me peace, which I employed,

not in bodily or worldly ease, but in meditation, that I might look on the world from afar, and contemplate a little the secrets of heaven.

11. O dearest and most beautiful Beloved, I beseech Thee to take me under Thy care, when Thou seest me assailed by any sinful temptation, or occupied by any vain affairs, that I may not begin to wander far from Thee after a crowd of foolish thoughts. For Thou art my Lord and my God, who healest and sanctifiest all things by Thy word, who hast placed my soul in life, and hast not allowed my feet to be moved, but didst draw me in an evil time from the snares of death.

12. How many have been forsaken and have perished who were more innocent than I am! Therefore bless the Lord, my soul, and all that is within thee praise His holy name. My soul, bless the Lord, and be not forgetful of His goodness.

13. Whatever you think or say or promise in praise of Him is indeed small and very little, for He is above all praise, and sweeter than every melody. Therefore does my soul cling to Thee, and love Thee above all Thy gifts, though they be precious and sweet, which in Thy charity Thou sendest to me.

14. Thou alone art my Spouse ; all Thy gifts are but pledges of Thy love ; I will not love them above Thee, nor will I imagine that all things are sufficient for me without Thee, lest perhaps I should lose Thee together with them.

15. Thou permittest me to use many things for Thee, but Thou deniest me to enjoy them without Thee. Therefore, my beloved Spouse, Jesus Christ, I prefer Thee to all, and I will strive to love Thee above all. Grant, therefore, that I may happily enjoy Thee, and that in this enjoyable union I may be eternally beatified with Thee.

CHAPTER XIV

THE PRECEDING SUBJECT IS CONTINUED

1. THOUGH up to the present I may not have been good, yet I do not despair, nor will I despair, of becoming better. True and certain are the things narrated by the saints, who were exercised in many things, and proven by similar trials.

2. Nature always desires to be at ease, and seeks to be consoled, but the Spirit is ready to bear all things which God wishes me to suffer. If, therefore, I have been less fervent and prompt to do good, my fault will not be without its remedy. ' Even should He kill me, said the just, I will continue to hope in Him.' If I love virtues, patience is a great virtue, and let it still be practised.

3. The difficulty of doing good often adds lustre to virtue, for to be proven and often tried by many contradictions is to be rendered brighter as regards virtue. When, therefore, you experience

these trials, be not diffident or downcast, but preserve your patience, and commend yourself to the goodness of God.

4. God is not so unkind and unmerciful as to allow you for a long time to be without consolation. Beware, however, not to grieve immoderately, or to murmur against Him, who is just and holy, because you have been left to yourself; lest the malignant spirit assail you with greater temptations to blasphemy and against faith, of which being very much afraid, you may be tormented more than you should care.

5. Therefore, bear with yourself a little, and repress your grief, even though you suffer some pain in mind and body, and continue firm in your good resolution which you proposed to observe from the beginning. It helps very much in this circumstance to place all hope in your Beloved.

6. Expect patiently heavenly consolation, and you shall soon feel abundant grace and favour of God. Behold, you have a faithful witness, saying : ' Expecting, I have awaited the Lord, and He came to me.'

7. But that you may soon deserve to obtain this, pray often in the meantime, and ask others to pray for you. Commit yourself so completely to His will and providence as to ask Him to do with you what is pleasing to Him, and say with great confidence, ' My lot is in your hands.' You know how it is with me, you know what I suffer, and

l shall be quickly consoled if you now will. Let that be always done which is right and proper in Thy sight, and have pity on me, a poor desolate being humbly asking for help.

8. If, therefore, you persevere in patience and long-suffering, and on account of a few trials do not fall away from the faith and charity which are in Christ Jesus, the splendour of His grace will certainly return and give you more abundant light. The Beloved returning will be far dearer to you than if He had never been absent. His word is not irrevocable, nor is He so offended as not to be willingly reconciled. He is soon and easily appeased if you only endeavour to avoid offending Him, and to make what satisfaction you are able. If you comply with these salutary admonitions your Beloved will be with you as He was before, and you shall rejoice with His presence, and say, ' How great, O Lord, is the multitude of Thy sweetness, which Thou hast hidden for those that fear Thee. Thou hast done much for them that hope in Thee, and Thou wilt protect them under the cover of Thy wings.' O Sion, thou shalt be renewed, and thou shalt see thy illustrious King, who will reign in thee. Thy Beloved is the King of virtues, whose hinder parts are the paleness of gold, and whose head is the purest gold.

CHAPTER XV

CONFIDENCE IN DIVINE MERCY

' I have not come to call the just, but sinners.'—MARK ii. 17.

1. Is it not lawful for Me to do what I will ? Who will resist My will ? If I wish to do a little good to you, though the last, who will accuse Me of sin ? He who is without sin, let him first cast a stone at thee, for if they are sinners, why do they deprive themselves of grace ? You have not chosen Me, but My mercy went before you.

2. You should justly despise yourself, and never forget in how many things you have sinned, but you should not be over-despondent. Think how often I change sinners into just men and friends, choosing the humble and abandoning those who presume on themselves. I have no need that you give Me anything, but this only do I require, and it suffices, that you love Me with a pure heart. Are not all things mine—those that adorn your body and beautify your mind ?

3. You did justly humble and accuse yourself in thought and in word before the face of My majesty by truly confessing your weakness and sinfulness, and by sincerely grieving for them, for you are unworthy to claim even for a moment the grace of My friendship, I being the mirror of purity, and you a sinner defiled from infancy.

4. Be therefore mindful of your frail condition, and of My greatness, that you may confidently approach Me with humble reverence. I am He who blots out iniquity and sins, who justifies the wicked by forgiving him all his crimes on account of My name, I prefer mercy to anger, I desire to spare rather than to punish.

5. But this seems little to Me, and I am not content with it, but after the first grace I add a second and a third. Indeed, I place no limit to My mercies, and My graces and benefits are beyond number. For after the pardon of sins, after penance, and full satisfaction, I often bestow the joy of My saving countenance, and pour into the soul more abundant graces of the Holy Ghost.

6. Though the sinner is still detained in the flesh, yet I receive him into My friendship, so that he needs not to have any shame of his past sins; but he should be full of gratitude and praise that the old things have passed away, and all are made new.

7. I am so clement and merciful that I am always more prepared to forgive than you to repent, more ready to give than you to ask. Why, therefore, do you fear ? Why do you tremble to approach the fountain of so great piety ? And why do you keep away from My grace, which is so freely offered to you ?

8. If you even knew that I had intended to refuse you should not desist from asking, nor

lose confidence of being heard, but much more earnestly pray till you shall be heard, for My mercies are infinite, and what may be at one time denied can at another time be granted.

9. Who knows when I will turn My face to you, and give the desire of your heart ? For what says the prophet of me ?—'Draw near to Him, and be enlightened, and your face shall not be confounded.'

10. I complain of the rarity rather than of the frequency of your approach to Me, and of your timid diffidence more than the hopeful confidence of pardon. Confidence in My goodness is a sign of true humility and great faith. This I say, do not sin, but should you sin do not despair, but quickly rise, for you have even then hope, and an Advocate with the Father.

11. Do you expect to be worthy before you approach Me ? And when shall you be worthy by your own efforts ? If only the good and worthy, the great and perfect, should approach Me, to whom should the publicans and sinners go ? What does the Gospel say ?—the publicans and sinners came to Jesus to hear Him.

12. The unworthy should therefore approach Him that they may be made worthy, the bad that they may become good, the little and imperfect that they may grow great and perfect. Let all and each approach that they may receive from the abundance of the living Fountain. I am the fountain of life which cannot be exhausted.

He who thirsts, let him come to Me and drink, and he who has nothing, let him come and purchase without money.

13. He who is sick, let him come to be cured; he who is tepid, let him come to be made fervent. Let the timid come to be encouraged, the sorrowful to be consoled, the parched to be filled with the riches and graces of the Spirit, and the grieved to be filled with gladness.

14. Indeed, My delight is to be with the sons of men. He who desires wisdom, let him come to learn My doctrine; he who seeks riches, let him come to receive those that are incorruptible and inexhaustible; he who goes after honours, let him come to inherit an eternal name in heaven; he who seeks happiness, let him come to possess it without fear or danger; and he who desires the abundance of every good, let him come to Me, that he may enjoy the eternal and infinite good,

15. I am He who gives all temporal goods, and besides the temporal I bestow eternal in heaven. Never do I go back of My promises when the salutary observance of My commands is fulfilled. He shall be gloriously crowned in heaven who has legitimately fought on earth.

END OF BOOK I

BOOK II

WHAT THINGS CAN BE TRULY AND JUSTLY CALLED GOOD AND BAD

CHAPTER I

THE SHORTNESS AND MISERIES OF THE PRESENT LIFE

'Declare unto me the fairness of my days.'—Ps. ci.

1. So long as I am in the world I shall not be free from sin, and so long as I remain here I shall be a poor pilgrim and sojourner on the earth. I brought nothing into the world, and I shall take nothing out of it; for I came into it naked, and I shall depart from it in the same state, and shall leave it as a lodger of one night. The whole present life is one short night. My days are few and evil, and shall soon be at an end.

2. The remembrance of man on earth is short, both to those who knew him and to those who knew him not; but the just shall be in eternal remembrance, because he shall be always united to God, who never dies. He is therefore happy who does not place his hope in man, and does not over-rejoice in anything of the world or in its

47

appearances, but who has his heart fixed on heaven, because everything here is vain and deceitful.

3. Call to mind all men from the beginning of the world to the present time, and tell me, I beseech you, where are they? And those whom you now see and hear, how long do you think they shall remain? Say, therefore, of all, every living man is vanity, and life poor and miserable, frail and lamentable, which the good suffer rather than love, and the bad, though they love it much, cannot long live in it.

4. O widespread vanity of the world, when will you end? When will you finish? But the time will come when all the elect, who often mourn because they are far from the kingdom of Christ, shall be delivered from the slavery of corruption. Oh that the whole world would wither in my heart, and that I could possess only my sweet Lord, my immortal Spouse!

5. The passing pleasure of this life is indeed a bitter cup, and the more one becomes inebriated with it, the more he feels its tortures, because all the joys of this world pass by quicker than the wind, and leave sorrows and pains to their lovers. Depart, therefore, from me the deceitful glory of the world, and all its false and carnal pleasures. Come and approach me, holy abnegation, and the entire contempt of all the pomps of the world, and do not depart from me the salutary remembrance of my pilgrimage.

6. Oh how miserable I have become, and how justly I may grieve; when I consider my pilgrimage, I am ignorant how it will end. If I shall have lived well, and shall have persevered in goodness, then I will not fear a bad death. O Lord God of my salvation, give a good end of my life. Weeping I came into this prison, and I shall not depart from it without fear.

7. This life, which causes frequent misery and sadness, appears to me long; but indeed it is not long, and the time runs by quicker than courier. Every time is long to him who is in sadness and grief, and he counts a day a year. This life is so wearisome that the more thoughtfully I consider it the more grievously it affects me.

8. But though some consolations and joys intervene, it behoves me to examine whether they come from God or not. If from God, I willingly accept them, but I do not know how long they may last. However, they are pleasing and agreeable to me, how small soever they may be, and would, O my God, that they flowed more abundantly, and continued longer with me.

9. But those that are not from God are vile and soon pass away, though in appearance they seem sweet and pleasant. Thus passes this life, always mixed with good and bad things. Therefore, so long as I am here I am a poor pilgrim. I cannot say I am satisfied, for the satiety of any good is not to be enjoyed at present. But Thou,

O Lord, art my good, whom I expect and in whom I hope.

10. When, however, Thy glory shall appear, and shall have filled me, then I will confess to Thee, for I shall be fully satisfied. But in the meantime, as this is hidden from me, my soul is surrounded by many trials. Therefore I will bear in mind Thy holy word, and say, ' My soul is sorrowful even unto death.' It will be good when this time shall have passed, and when no grief or sorrow shall oppress me. But I pray, O Lord, that Thy clemency may preserve me.

CHAPTER II

THE PRECEDING SUBJECT CONTINUED

' Watch, because ye know not the day or the hour.'— MATT. xxv.

1. HAPPY the soul that often thinks of the last hour, when all things in this life shall cease—joy and sadness, honour and contempt. Happy is the poor soul that became a pilgrim for God, and despised all worldly grandeur, be it ever so great and splendid.

2. In that last hour shall perish all castles, villas, towns, all gold and silver vessels, sumptuous furniture, and various vases scented with spices. Then shall also cease the harp, trumpet, flute, guitar, all plays, jests, laughter, dancing, rejoicing and singing, all music and hilarity in

the squares and houses, for the hearts of all shall be brought to nothing, all, all the earth shall fear before the face of the Lord.

3. Blessed is he who willingly abandons all things that would give pleasure to the flesh in this world, which is full of snares and dangers. Blessed is the pilgrim who often sighs and grieves in this exile, and desires to be dissolved, and to be with Christ in the heavenly kingdom. Blessed is he who hates the world, and all those things which entice to sin, and who flees with Elias into the desert from the presence of many evils that often draw the unguarded into hell. Blessed is he who watches night and day against his temptations, and often prays with Elias, saying, ' It is sufficient, O Lord ; take away my soul.' It is better for me to die with good hope, and to depart from this life in grace, than to witness evils, and to live in the midst of dangers.

4. He therefore is very much deceived, and errs like a fool who desires to live long in this world, and proposes to do many things, but does not know whether he shall be alive to-morrow. Call to your mind a man, noble, rich, and enjoying every pleasure. What shall he be when buried in the earth after death ? What then do riches and pleasures profit him ?

5. Behold to-day the King lives and commands, to-morrow he is neither seen nor heard ; to-day he is seated upon an elevated throne and covered with a golden mantle, to-morrow he is buried

under earth and no longer seen; to-day he is
honoured by many, to-morrow he is cared for by
none; to-day he is magnified by all, to-morrow
he is deprived of riches and honours, villas and
castles; to-day he is most charming among men
and in the number of Kings, to-morrow he is the
food of worms and offensive to our smell. As
he came into the world naked, so as a pauper and
exile he is borne to the grave.

6. All the pleasures and pomps of the world
shall soon end. What is the whole time of our
life, unless the present short instant, as the wind
blowing by, as the dawn passing in the morning,
as the lodger not returning? As the lightning of
heaven in the twinkling of the eye, so do all the
kingdoms and ages of the world perish. Count
up all the hours, days, months, and years of your
life, and tell me where are they now? They
have passed away as a shadow, they have perished
as a spider's web, for the wind blew and its work
was destroyed. Nothing, therefore, is firm or
durable upon the earth from which Adam and
his sons were formed.

7. Whatever in the world appears beautiful
and delightful is vain and perishable. Let not,
therefore, pleasures deceive you, nor injuries dis-
hearten you. No matter how much one may be
adorned with colours, and decorated with gold,
silver, and precious stones, he becomes vile and
reduced to dust in the grave. Therefore in every
work you do, in whatever place you are, wither-

soever you go and wheresoever you pass, be mindful of the end of your life, and of your last hour, of which you are ignorant.

8. He is happy who desires with Paul to be dissolved and to be with Christ, for this is much better than to live longer in the flesh, to be a pilgrim from God, and to be struck and knocked about by the storms of this world.   If you always bear Jesus in your mind, and daily pray to Him, then indeed you shall have confidence in the kingdom of Him who said, ' I will, O Father, that where I am, there also shall My ministers be.'   Blessed is the servant who shall deserve to hear on the last day, ' Well done, thou good and faithful servant, because thou hast been faithful over a few things, enter into the joy of thy Lord.'

CHAPTER III

SIGHING FOR ETERNAL LIFE

' Bring out of prison my soul.'—Ps. cxli.

1. THE force of grief does not allow me to be silent, for why do I delay here longer ?   Thou wilt do me a great favour, O Lord, if Thou wilt soon take me hence, lest I should become worse. My life, which does not become better in works, is spent in grief.

2. How negligently and tepidly I act !   Why do I unworthily and without profit occupy the

place of one whose life would be better ?   I often
turn over in my mind and seriously think on this
sad subject ; but, O good God, do not in anger
pronounce against me this sentence, ' Cut down
the tree, and cast it into the fire!'

3. I acknowledge my weakness, and confess it
to Thee, that Thou mayest pardon me.   It is my
duty to accuse myself, it is Thy mercy to pardon ;
it is my place to sincerely grieve and weep, it is
Thy goodness to kindly console the weeper.
Therefore, O Lord, either grant me greater grace
in this life, or take me soon from the world, lest
the separation becomes greater.

4. To live longer and not to amend my life is
to increase my punishment.   A life that makes no
proficiency in virtue, and does not weep for its
deficiencies, cannot be pleasing to Thee.   He
who lives holily and justly grieves for all those
things in which he fails, and he has always the
desire to increase in virtue and in grace.   But
what shall he do who is conscious that he fails
every day, and feels the flesh obstinately resisting
the spirit ?

5. He who is sometimes overcome by weariness
and becomes tepid from waste of time ceases
to fight, or, laying down his spiritual armour,
follows the impulse of the flesh according as his
self-will draws him.   Alas ! such a one, O Lord,
draws nearer to the gates of death, and by
following the flesh incurs the death of the soul.

6. Oh how each should fear the snares and

deceits of the enemy! No one is safe, no one is free from sin, but all are frail. Thou, O Lord, who canst do all things, and knowest all things, comfort the broken-hearted, purify the unclean, and give a new spirit, that all torpor and languidness may depart and spiritual fervour may return, and thy love may be constant to the end.

7. Never let my heart rejoice according to the flesh, but let it expect death with fear. Let no creature or business lay hold of me, but let Thy desirable presence draw and console me. Blessed is he who expects Thee, O Lord, but more blessed is he who has already departed from this wicked world, for never more shall he feel or fear any unhappiness.

CHAPTER IV

THE ETERNAL PRAISE OF GOD, DIVINE LOVE, AND DESIRE OF ETERNAL GLORY

1. 'O MY SOUL, praise the Lord,' from whom every good proceeds, now and for ever. You should therefore refer all things to Him, at the beginning and end of every action, and with great gratitude sincerely praise Him, that the gifts of heavenly grace may more abundantly flow into your soul, till you come to the fountain of everlasting life, to the country of eternal splendour, and to the sight of the Divine presence and glory.

2. You can do nothing more salutary, sweeter, more joyful, more worthy, higher, happier, more perfect, or more blessed, than to love and praise God ardently. This I say one hundred times; this I repeat one thousand times—there is no study more sublime, no work more eminent, than to love and praise God, your Creator and Redeemer, with your whole heart, with your whole soul, with your whole mind, and with your entire strength. Do this so long as you live, feel, and understand; accomplish this by word and work, by night and day, at morning, noon, and evening, at every hour and at every moment.

3. According to your knowledge and ability be entirely and purely united to God, that He may be all in all, before all, and above all; that He may be loved, blessed, praised, and exalted by you, that you may be with Him for ever. Exult, therefore, O faithful soul, in the Lord your God, as the Blessed Virgin Mary exulted in Jesus her Saviour. Exult and praise your God, who created and redeemed you. You are a debtor to Him for very many and great benefits, for the daily gifts He kindly gives you, for all which, though you were a holy angel, you cannot fully and worthily thank Him. Nevertheless, O mortal man, needing the mercy of God, and always seeking and imploring it, praise and give Him thanks. Cease not to pray and praise Him.

4. Though you may often fall and offend God,

do not therefore despair; but humble yourself
the more and pray. Love, and you shall be
loved, because love makes amends for all past
falls. It purifies, it heals, it enlightens and inflames, it drives away sadness, and it brings to
the heart joy which the world does not know, and
flesh and blood do not understand.

5. Praise God, and you shall be praised; bless,
and you shall be blessed; sanctify, and you shall
be sanctified; magnify, and you shall be magnified; glorify God, and you shall be glorified by
Him in soul and body. But when will this be,
O Lord? When wilt Thou fill my mouth with
constant praise? When shall my heart and soul
exult with Thy saints in glory?

6. O Lord, my Saviour, and my God, when
wilt Thou make me joyful in Thy kingdom
with the splendour of Thy countenance? Oh,
when wilt Thou enlighten my darkness with the
brightness of eternal light? When wilt Thou
take away from the midst of my heart all my
defects? When shall I enjoy true peace, com-
plete blessedness, and perfect happiness? Oh,
when without any hindrance from obstacles shall
I securely and freely follow Thee, O Lord, whithersoever Thou goest?

7. Oh, when shall I know all that which I
believe in the Holy Scriptures, which I read in
various books, which I hear in many places from
lectures on God, on the angels, on all the chorus
of holy spirits, on the glory and blessedness of

the heavenly country, and on the peace and unspeakable joy of the citizens of Thy kingdom ?

8. Oh, when shall I be there ? When shall I
come and appear in Thy sight, contemplate Thy
joyful countenance, and the glory of Thy kingdom, with the cherubim, seraphim, and all the
saints ? But that hour has not yet come ; the
gate of heaven is yet closed against me. Therefore, so long as I am here, I will grieve in heart
and by word till my God comes to me.

CHAPTER V

DIVINE HOPE

'O Lord, Thou art my hope from my youth.'—Ps. lxx.

1. In this hope I will have recourse to Thee, till the
last hour, and till the time of my dissolution shall
have come. Oh that I may be well prepared, and
able to die in the hope of grace. Oh, from how
many dangers and fears shall I then escape, if I
end the last day and lay aside the burden of this
body by a happy death. Happy is he whom
Thou hast chosen and taken, who after death
passes from this world to the Father, from exile
to a kingdom, from a prison to a palace, from
darkness to light, from death to life, from danger
to safety, from labour to rest, and from all misery
to never-ending happiness.

2. Happy soul that is now in possession of its

reward, rejoicing in Thee, the Lord its God. But, ah me! because my sojourn is prolonged even till now. How graciously and mercifully Thou wouldst act to me, if Thou wouldst soon call me hence, and allow me to come to Thee, that where Thou art there also I may be.

3. I know as yet I am not well prepared, but I will firmly renew my desire, I will deplore my past negligences, I will devote myself entirely to Thee, and I will always commend myself to Thy mercy. O Lord God, all my works abide in Thy mercy; they are not meritorious of themselves, unless joined to Thy immense piety and goodness, and in this is my hope and entire confidence.

4. But how is it with a good and pure conscience? What says the chaste and devout soul? Come, it says, Lord Jesus, come and do not delay; pardon my faults, loose the chains, lead forth the bound from prison, from the abyss of misery, and from the filthy mire. Expecting, I have expected Thee; be attentive to me, and hear me. Grant me to now possess my desired joy, which has no limit, and is not darkened by any grief.

5. Show me Thy face, which the angels always see. Let Thy voice, which they hear without intermission, sound in my ears. Come, Lord Jesus, and take me from a strange land; call back the exile to his country; restore to the fallen his former place. Come, good Redeemer, and make me a partaker of Thy eternal glory.

6. It is time I should return to Thee, it is time Thou wouldst commit my body to earth, from which it was taken. It matters little where it is placed, or how it is treated, whilst the soul is saved, and returns to Thee. May my soul, which I commend to Thee, be happy; let my body rest in hope, to be reanimated at the last day. For wherever it may be placed, it cannot be hidden or unknown to Thee. Receive me and unite me to the society of the saints.

7. I am weary of my temporal life; the day of eternal beauty only delights me. Let not the old serpent oppose me on my departure from Egypt, let not the enemy rage against me at the gate, let not his terrible image frighten me, or the fear of death disturb me. But let Thy holy angels faithfully assist me, bravely help me, powerfully protect me, kindly and lovingly receive me, and with joy lead me to the heavenly paradise. May the Virgin Mary, the glorious Mother of God, assist me with all the saints.

8. And Thou, O good Jesus, sweet and lovely, give me the joy of Thy countenance, and do not reject me from Thy beloved saints, but remember and consider that Thou hast redeemed me from the enemy by Thy precious blood. Receive me in Thy mercy and goodness, because with desire I have desired to make this Pasch with Thee.

9. Oh happy day of my desired reward, Oh blessed hour of my happy departure, which I have long desired, and kept before my eyes.

What injury did the trials and sufferings in the world do me ? What harm came to me from contempt, labour, and humiliation for Thy name ? Thou hadst given me life, but now it is my gain to die, and to be with Thee in Thy kingdom will be a much greater good. To Thee be praise and glory, who art the life of the living, the hope of the dying, and the salvation and rest of all who come to Thee.

CHAPTER VI

CHRIST IS THE LIFE OF HIM WHO HAS DIED TO THE WORLD

' Turn away my eyes that they see not vanity.'—Ps. cxviii.

1. O JESUS, true life, the life that knows not death, grant that I may be absorbed in Thy love, wounded with Thy love, and die of Thy love, that the flesh may not rule over me. As yet I am not dead to the world, but the old man still lives in me, stirring up various desires, and truly making the days sorrowful and nights troublesome.

2. Oh, when will it come that I shall say with confidence, ' I indeed considered myself as one dead upon the earth '? For he who is dead cares not for the praises of men or for the reproaches of the upbraiding, because he is dead. He who is dead to the flesh does not anything wrong, hears not the vanity of the world, sees not the

curious and pleasant, or whatever could draw
him to love anything vile upon the earth.

3. He who is dead to the world is not in the
world, but in God, for whom he lives. As
St. Paul said to his beloved disciple, 'You are
dead, and your life is hidden with Christ in God.'
Such a one so speaks, thinks, and sees those things
which appear as if they were not, because those
things that are seen are temporal and vain, and
those which are not seen are eternal.

4. Therefore to these he looks, for these he sighs,
in these he has his heart, for these he labours,
and desires to reach them. He makes much of
them, he loves them, he seeks them, he finds
pleasure in the internal and hidden—namely, in
the great good, in the supreme good, in the eternal
good, of whom he cannot sufficiently think. Such
a one is very far distant from present things,
desires eternal joys with his whole affection, and
holds in subjection the sensual appetite.

5. For sensuality seeks exterior things, desires
pleasures, looks to what is present, neglects the
future, avoids whenever it can what is bitter and
disagreeable, though often profitable to the spirit.
Hence it does not allow the spirit to be in silence
and at rest, but brings before it various imaginations, difficult to be named, but which should
not be considered.

6. But he who has the grace of spiritual forti-
tude is able to subdue quickly the insolent
motions of the flesh by pronouncing the word of

Divine power : ' The Lord is my helpér : I will not fear what the flesh may do to me.' Therefore, though sensuality may cause trouble to him, and the voice of the flesh may murmur, yet he does not easily consent, because greater by far is the force of God's love, which interiorly strengthens him.

7. Such a one is sometimes so sweetly, strongly, and ardently drawn to God, captured and held, that he does not see, and scarcely feels, what is present, or what takes place in the world, because he is not there, but elsewhere. He is not below with himself, but above with God, and in God, who inwardly moves, elevates, and, as it were, carries him away in a fiery chariot, that he may sometimes enjoy Him by holy desire in the happy and ardent aspirations of his heart.

8. He considers these things with himself, and is lost in admiration with so great a good that surpasses all reason, and is greater than any gift. He again wonders and earnestly asks, What is this ? And he rejoices exceedingly, because manna has descended from heaven.

9. But He who supplies true bread from heaven gives also right understanding to him who tastes it, that he may know ' that every best and perfect gift is from above, descending from the Father of men.' This word, he says, is indeed from God. I have all things from Him, and nothing without Him. Again, he wonders and laments why he cares so little for so great good, which

brought him immense happiness. Why also he does not incline his heart often to hear and see it, than which nothing sweeter or happier can be enjoyed.

10. And oh that it may continue, for it gives me great pleasure, and will give me more if I attend to it. Let my Beloved come into my heart, that I may eat of His fruit; let Him turn towards me, and show Himself to me, and I to Him. Then he begins to long for, to desire, and to ardently love the good, in whom is every good; the joy, in whom is every joy; the only one in whom are all, the little and great, the high and low.

11. Hence he sometimes wishes to be entirely filled with this good, to be inundated with this sweetest joy, and to be wholly absorbed and consumed, in order to satisfy his insatiable love, so that he has nothing of himself, but is entirely His who has given him this intense love, and wrought this wonderful work by which he is wrapped up in his Beloved and become one spirit with Him. He should not on this account exalt himself, or think anything of himself, or despise others, or look down on those less favoured, because this is not his doing, but the gratuitous gift of God. It is therefore just that he should not extol himself when he perceives that he is so consoled.

12. For he neither seeks praises nor cares for external favours, but he seeks his Beloved, and

desires only His praise and approbation, in whom he has all, and in whom he finds all; for His love, His sweetness, His joyful function is preferable to all transitory things, and therefore he desires and loves His honour above all.

13. He should not therefore think highly of himself, or foolishly glory in any good. The Beloved is his glory, his praise, his exultation, his true and sincere joy, his great and only good, his whole desire and satisfaction. He should rather wish that others rejoice with himself, and possess the same good without end, now and for ever.

14. Let him desire and pray that his Beloved make himself known to all men, that He convert and draw all to Himself, that He alone be praised and glorified, as He loves all more than He can be loved by them. It is therefore pleasing to Him that each desires to sincerely love Him, though he may not possess intense love, for He surpasses and conquers all in love.

CHAPTER VII

WITHDRAWING FROM CREATURES

'Lo, I have gone far off, flying away, and I abode in the wilderness.'—Ps. liv.

1. How salutary, how pleasant, how sweet to sit in solitude, to be silent, to speak with God, and to enjoy Him alone, the greatest good, in whom

5

is every good! 'Unhappy man, who will deliver me from the body of this death?' Alas! how often does my soul draw near death on account of creatures which it loves. It often forgets the Creator for them, and is drawn away from Him. My mind is inconstant; now it desires this, then that; now it is here, then there, seeking peace in creatures, and not finding it.

2. Though every creature has some pleasure in its use, yet it cannot give contentment in its enjoyment. The heart of man is inscrutable, and who knows it? Thou, O God, who knows the thoughts of man, for they are vain. O eternal God, great and immense, the Creator and ruler of all things, I am Thy creature whom Thou hast made by Thy power.

3. I am made to love Thee, and I desire to love Thee, but I cannot do it as I wish. I am bound by vain love and vicious affections for passing things from which I strive to free myself, but I cannot unless with great difficulty and much grief. Oh, if Thou wouldst give me Thy sweetness and pleasure, they would soon disappear and perish.

4. I sometimes see by a glance of the mind Thy hidden things, and Thee also, O greatest good, true and eternal God, by the things that are made. It delights me to rest in Thee, but immediately, moved by I know not what spirit, I am drawn from Thy contemplation by the love and attraction of visible things.

5. For in truth I have firmly proposed as a treaty between me and Thee that I will not behold or love any creature in preference to Thy noble and precious love. And after this thoughts come into my mind, showing me the joyful appearances of the world, but concealing the sad end ; exhibiting what is present, but silent about the evil that is to follow.

6. How vain, how deceitful and worthless are things which are present, and even flourishing, for they disappear after a short pleasure, and leave me among the thorns and pricks of a bad conscience! Woe to me, O Lord, and again woe to me, because I quickly believed and consented to vanity, but Thee, who art the Truth, I easily abandoned.

7. How grievously did I offend in not having clung to Thee in preference to all others. Have I not been created to love and enjoy Thee? but I have lost Thee by inordinately following creatures in which I found no peace of heart.

CHAPTER VIII

CONTEMPT FOR ALL EARTHLY CONSOLATION

'My soul refused to be consoled.'—Ps. lxxvi.

1. Do not, my soul, wander after vanities and foolish excuses, but turn to the Lord thy God, because He is the source of every consolation.

Whatever you shall find in men or in creatures you shall lose and feel the loss, because whatever consolation may appear in them cannot be lasting.

2. Why do you deceive yourself without reason ? It is foolish to beg from a pauper, when He who is rich wishes to give abundantly. Every creature is poor in giving consolation, but God is rich in grace, Who gives abundantly and does not reproach, provided you seek diligently and expect patiently.

3. Return, my soul, as did the dove to Noe, who brought it into the ark—return to Christ in the interior of your heart, because it is not safe for you to remain abroad. Refuse exterior consolation, if you wish to be refreshed with interior.

4. Many are the snares laid for the soul willingly wandering abroad. Great caution was used by the dove by quickly returning, ' which when it could not find where to rest its feet, it returned to Noe into the ark.' Blessed is the soul whose conscience is clear before God, and does not seek consolation from any creature, but places all its hope in God.

5. Blessed is the soul that refuses all external and temporal ease, and whatever relates to the comfort of the flesh, and willingly embraces labour and work for Christ. Blessed is the soul that commits itself to God, that He may do with it as He pleases.

6. Blessed is the soul that never seeks its own

glory, never desires to do its own will, but proposes, intends, and loves the will and glory of God
in all things. Happy and blessed by God is the
soul whose desires are towards heaven, whose
every effort and interior labour goes forth,
ascends, and does not return, till it finds Him
whom alone it loves above all ; and when it shall
have found Him, it forgets all others and follows
Him, wherever the Beloved wishes to conduct it.

7. When the Beloved will speak, the soul will
rejoice at His voice, saying, I am Thy beloved,
Thy only one, Thy chosen one ; ' I am Thy
reward exceeding great.' Be humble in prosperity, be brave in adversity.

8. Ah ! if I could enjoy such sweetness as a holy
soul, beloved by God and devoted to Him, enjoys,
when, the senses being suspended, it is borne
upwards in spirit, and raised above itself in the
contemplation of God, and united to Him by the
bond of intimate love ! O my God, the true
treasure of my heart, Thou knowest that the
sorrow hidden in my heart is my only refuge.

9. But Thou art the giver and infuser of this
sweetness ; Thou teachest and exhortest, caressest
and consolest, movest and sustainest, leadest
on and drawest back. Thou doest with the soul
what Thou chosest and pleasest, and all is good
whatever Thou wishest and doest. But as I am
a sour vessel, unworthy of the infusion of Thy
good Spirit, I beg an inflowing of it, that I may be
able to taste the sweetness of Thy internal love,

and feel those holy delights which I hope the soul, faithfully serving Thee, often merits.

10. Sometimes, however, in seeking the way of interior things, I have seriously considered in my meditations the graces given to a chosen soul, the many heavenly joys and spiritual delights, the peace and tranquillity of heart, the hope and exultation in God its Saviour, whose word is sweet and countenance beautiful. And though the time of its enjoyment may be short, yet it is agreeable.

11. In thinking of these things, I was enlightened to discover just complaints of myself, and to perceive by the hidden inlets of grace that a soul intimately united to Thee is such that Thou thus speakest to it. It is silent about all sensible things, and Thou speakest to it of invisible ; it seems as if it were abandoned by all creatures, but Thou consolest it in wonderful ways.

12. Again I said in my heart, Woe to the sinful soul, to the burdened conscience, to the tepid in conversation, to one not having the light of grace or spiritual consolation, and seeking tears and not finding any !

13. Peace to the one that sincerely loves Christ, and never turns from Him the eyes of its soul, but always seeks what is pleasing to Him ; for it will walk in peace and justice, and a stranger shall not partake of its joy. It will see that His peace is good, and it will be delighted, because the Lord its God, in whom it confides, is sweet.

14. The soul will withdraw itself from external tumults, and will expect with profit the coming of the Lord into the heart. Thus does God act towards His elect. If anyone will come to Him, he shall not go away empty, for He is willing to give drink to the thirsty and food to the hungry.

15. My God, when Thou comest into a soul loving Thee, dost Thou not nourish it with Thy milk, and leadest it sometimes even outside itself by Thy abundant sweetness, in order to know Thee without any corporal image? O Truth, O Truth, how great and powerful is Thy love! Then Thou secretly communicatest to the soul Thy word, and showest it all things, the old and the new, in love and happy enjoyment, where all human language ceases. From that time Thou principally treatest of eternal rest and of the society of the saints, with the soul confiding in Thee, because, desiring very much a pledge of spiritual favour, Thou renderest it more qualified to hope for those things it does not see, and to despise those that are present and by which it is held by the senses. O good Father, remember, in Thy mercy, me a poor beggar, and send me the true bread from heaven—the good word full of consolation and grace.

CHAPTER IX

THAT GREAT SWEETNESS AND CONSOLATION ARE FOUND IN GOD

'All my bones shall say, Who is like to Thee, O Lord.'—— Ps. xxxiv.

1. THOU art my only one, O my God, and who is like to Thee ?   Everything compared to Thee is nothing, my intimate Beloved, my most Faithful Friend, who never deserts him who loves Thee, and who willingly associates Himself to him who loves Thee.

2. And if sometimes He withdraws Himself, and permits me to be tried, He does it, not to reject, but to try, to purify, and enlighten me. He does not by any means desert, but wisely instructs, that it may be seen what one really is, and how far he is advanced.

3. Thou art beautiful, my Beloved, and most lovable, not to the flesh, but to the mind ; not to the sight or any sense, but to the soul believing in Thee, having a pure heart, and giving itself to invisible and spiritual things.   Whoever, therefore, desires to be united to Thee in the spirit of devotion should mortify in himself every carnal affection, and watchfully attend to the purity of his conscience.

4. He who goes after frail creatures to seek consolation displeases Thee.   Therefore Thou invitest me internally to love Thee, Thou commandest me

to expect Thee, for then I shall find Thee as often as I deny myself. As Thou willest, so do I.

5. And this will be my entire good, to reverence and serve Thee purely, fearing neither loss nor gain for Thy love, because Thou commandest the soul that purely loves Thee. Oh happy one in life and death united to Thee alone ! I often go by another way in loving perishable things, not as I should, nor as becomes my end.

6. But that I may not perish with them, I will quickly return, by considering Thy glory in them, and by directing my affections to Thee. Thou Lord my God, who made all from nothing, grant that all may praise Thy holy name, for Thou art powerful, wise, good, clement, and Thy Majesty and glory are eternal. Thy kingdom is the kingdom of all ages, and Thy power is from generation to generation. Thou disposest all things in heaven and on earth.

7. Thou knowest all, Thou holdest all in Thy hands : nothing resists Thee, nothing disturbs Thee ; Thou judgest all in tranquillity, and Thou subjectest the rebellious, and makest them serve Thee. Thou knowest all that is being done in the universe, and even before they are being done, and Thou didst bring them to their proper end. Thou art the God of heaven and earth, the Creator and Director of visible and invisible things, and the Disposer of all times. Preserve, I beseech Thee, Thy servants dispersed through the length and breadth of the world, especially those deputed

to Thy service, and so order that they narrate Thy praises, and with united voice everywhere proclaim Thy glory. Stir up in their hearts an ardent love for Thee, and enable them to bring all Thy holy works to a happy end.

8. Oh, how clement and sweet Thou art to those who love Thee! how very pleasing to those who taste Thy sweetness! Those who have experienced it know they cannot think or speak of anything better. Thy sweetness surpasses all pleasure, and renders pleasant all that is disagreeable.

9. O Lord my God, holy men have spoken of Thee, and Thy prophets were not silent of Thee; all the saints from the beginning of the world believed in Thee, served Thee, and worshipped Thee with sacrifices and offerings; they praised and blessed Thy name, because they knew Thee to be the Creator and Ruler of all things, and they hoped in Thee above all.

10. They knew Thee in Thy visitation, for Thou didst reveal to them Thy name, and they knew no other but Thee. They kept the law of Thy commandments which Thou gavest them; they did not follow the vain images of false gods, but adored Thee, living from eternity, and who created all things. They raised up their voice in confession of Thy praise, because Thou from on high didst put into their hearts these great words, ' I am who I am : before Me, God was not formed, nor will be after Me.' I made those

things which exist, and the past has not been forgotten by Me.

11. Hearing and understanding these things, they raised up even from afar the eyes of faith, believing that the Lord will save us, that He will come who was promised to come, and will not deceive. Foreknowing these things, they were greatly consoled, lost in astonishment, and very much wondered at the presence of His infinite Majesty ; but, taking breath a little, and with joy beholding the greatness of God coming to them, said, He is, He is the Lord our God, and He is no other ; He has begun, and He will save us ; He cannot deny Himself, for He is true.   This is the voice of the saints in my ears ; it is as honey at a banquet, and as incense diffusing its fragrance from the thurible, so is the word of God in a pure heart.

CHAPTER X

SEEKING THE ONLY AND BEST GOOD

'Say to my soul, I am thy salvation.'—Ps. xxxiv.

1. How noble thou art, my soul, and what a force is hidden in thee, for thou art not able to rest, unless in the possession of the greatest good. O good above every good, O end without end, when shall I enjoy Thee without measure and without end ?   I here find many things, but they are changeable, and do not satisfy me.

2. But One is necessary : this One I seek, this One I desire ; all things are on account of this One, all come from this One. If I shall have this One, I am content, and unless I shall possess it I am always dissatisfied, because all others cannot content me.

3. Who is this One ? I am unable to name Him, but I feel that I desire Him than whom no One can be thought better or greater. For this is not one among all, but One above all. He is my God, to whom to be joined and united is my good. To Him I will speak and cry out, Say to my soul, I am thy salvation.

4. What more do you wish, my soul that is full of desires ? Is it not better to be united to one than to many ? From this one you receive much, from many you do not possess Him. Cease to seek many, join yourself to one, be united to one, by whom all exist. Some seek many and various things from without ; you seek the one and internal good, which is sufficient for you.

5. Behold, one desires a villa, another applies himself to business, another amasses much gold and silver, another goes after pleasure and honours, another is attached to his friends and relations, another willingly visits his acquaintances and neighbours, another goes into towns and cities, another, led by curiosity, visits various parts of the world, another seeks wisdom, another power, another office, and another requires royal and princely homage.

6. Few purely and simply seek the One on account of Himself, and therefore they do not find lasting peace and do not feel internal grace. For whoever belong to Christ do not seek temporal and earthly things, imagining they should be great and glorious if they abounded in them.

7. It does not concern you, O devout soul, what others seek ; indeed, it is nothing to you. I detest all these things, because One is the good whom I love, One is the good whom I seek, and He is better to me than all others above and below.

8. If you have found this immense good, I exhort and beseech you to guard and keep Him for whom you have despised all things ; for, having Him, it will not be hard for you to want all ; rather you shall judge it right to give and suffer all in order to gain Him.

9. Therefore, my soul, seek this particular and supereminent good, and so long as you live cease not to seek Him, because He, who cannot be fully comprehended, cannot be sufficiently found. When the hour of possessing Him comes, then there will be an end of seeking Him. Then He will be all to all, for He alone will be sufficient for each and all. And if He is sought even there, where He is always found, it will not be with labour, as it is here, but with the greatest joy and love.

10. Consider a little, with the aid of experience guiding you, what are the names of Divine piety. I will mention a few, but grace may teach you

others more sacred. He is the Spouse to the loving, and to those who yet serve Him in fear He is the Lord to be feared. He is father to good sons, but to the bad a just judge. He is physician to the infirm, but solid food to the healthy. He is doctor to the ignorant, and eternal salvation to those who obey Him.

11. He is the way to beginners, truth to the proficient, and life to the perfect. He is the hope of penitents, and the supreme comforter of the just. He is the glory of the humble, and the punishment of the proud. He is light in darkness, and a lamp in the night.

12. He is present with those who fight, He walks with the proficient, He runs with the fervent, and He flies with the contemplative. He is present with those who pray, He speaks to those who read, and He rests with those who meditate.

13. In all these the one and the same God operates, appearing to each as He pleases. There is no rebuke in His word, and no questioning of His action ; just and unsearchable are His judgments, and no one can say, Why hast thou done this ? or, Why hast Thou chosen this one rather than that ? Foolish is the questioning of men about Omnipotence, and the research of the sons of Adam is vanity and nothing.

14. But as intense love is sometimes forgetful of reverence and fear, it is pardonable if the lover, now and then on fire for his Beloved, may ask, not only in what way the little Infant cries in the

manger and the Crucified hangs upon the cross, but also in what manner He gloriously reigns in heaven, and wonderfully disposes of all things on earth. My Jesus, to be beloved, I will follow Thee most willingly on earth, and I will much more willingly follow Thee in heaven.

15. Wheresoever my treasure is, there is also my heart. Thou art my treasure, dearer to me than every creature ; my eyes shall always be turned towards Thee, and my steps shall always follow Thee ; ' My heart hath said to Thee, My face hath sought Thee : thy face, O Lord, shall I still seek.'

16. Till now, O Lord, was the vision of Thy glory. ' Why hidest Thou Thy face, and thinkest me Thy enemy ?' Thou knowest that my soul has been for a long time borne hither and thither, and my affections have been drawn backwards and forwards to divers things (and so it will be), till I be joined to Thee, my Beloved, in heaven.

17. Draw me, and I will begin to fervently run after Thee. I have need of grace, and great grace. For unless you invite, no one comes, no one follows, for each is inclined to self-love. If Thou drawest me, behold I come, I hasten, I run, and I am on fire, but if Thou dost not, I neither run nor seek Thee, nor scarcely do I desire to follow Thee. But if Thou givest me Thy hand, I shall as swiftly run after Thee as Thou wilt efficaciously draw me.

18. This is the voice of my Beloved drawing

me : ' When I shall be exalted from the earth, I
will draw all things to Myself.' Good Jesus,
draw me after Thee, and not only me, but all,
following the odour of Thy fragrance; but first
draw me after Thee. This is the Divine attraction, without which no one advances, neither
does anyone begin, as Thou hast said : ' No one
cometh to Me unless My Father draws him.
Therefore whomsoever the Father draws, he
indeed follows Me and leaves himself.' ' Master,
I will follow Thee whithersoever Thou goest.'

19. What is the hindrance, my soul, that pre-
vents you from leaving all things for Jesus ?
Why do you so unwillingly separate yourself
from vain and perishable things ? In what do
these visible things help you ? For when you
follow those mortal and visible creatures, and
wish to be content with them, you lose those that
are better. When you do this, you separate
yourself from the greatest good, and turn yourself
away from the true, blessed, and eternal life.
Therefore you remain miserable and unhappy,
full of griefs and anxieties.

20. For whithersoever you intend to turn yourself, you shall always find sorrow and trouble,
unless you be converted to your Creator, because
He is your peace and safe repose. But if you do
not rest in earthly things, nor be attached to
them, but rather consider and reverence in
creatures, not their image, which passes away,
but Him whose likeness and superscription are

stamped upon them, you shall be happy, and shall live in grace.

21. But if you seek all visible things, not to enjoy them, but to look on them, in order to bless the name of your Creator, you make for yourself, as it were, from His little and great works, a ladder by which you raise and free yourself from this wicked world; then you shall be intimately joined to your desired end, God, who is above all and blessed for ever.   Amen.

CHAPTER XI

TRUE PEACE IS TO BE SOUGHT IN GOD ALONE

'Peace be to you, I am He, be not afraid.'—JOHN xxi.

1. ALL happiness and true peace of soul is in Christ Jesus.   He who loves Christ has peace and enjoys it.   Nor does he any longer strive after anything beyond or above Him.   The peace of a faithful soul in this world consists in bearing many contradictions for the love of God and in the name of Christ.

2. He is deceived and errs who feels and thinks otherwise.   He labours in vain who does not propose to himself God in his every thought and act, and who does not seek and desire Him purely.   The Lord says, 'There is no peace for the wicked'; and again, 'They who love Thy law, O Lord, have much peace.'

6

3. The peace which Christ taught and promised consists in profound humility, in the denial of one's will, in the mortification of every bad passion, in the rejection of worldly praise, and external consolation in perishable things. Guard, therefore, your heart from within, and your senses from without, that you may not be ensnared by any allurements or pleasures hurtful to your soul,

4. Creatures are often helpful if we directly and purely refer them to the praise and honour of God, or when we moderately and discreetly use them for our necessities, or for the benefit of others. But beautiful things are often hurtful if they be looked at curiously or impurely, or wrongly desired. All temporal things are defective and unendurable, and nothing is perfect but God, who is the greatest joy and the supreme good. If in Christ alone you seek peace and tranquillity of heart, His sweet and holy word shall be fulfilled in you, ' Blessed are the clean of heart, for they shall see God,' to whom be praise, honour, and glory from every creature for ever. Amen.

CHAPTER XII

THE DESIRE OF DIVINE ENJOYMENT

'The meditation of my heart is always in Thy sight.'—Ps. xxiii.

1. WHAT can be sweeter, what more pleasant, to the pious soul than to devoutly meditate on the Lord God, its Beloved ? As it cannot yet behold Him in the clear and beatific vision, it can at least have Him present, by a studious remembrance of Him.

2. As it cannot see Him face to face, let it, however, contemplate Him as in a glass, let Him be sought in the Scriptures and in figures, whom it cannot contemplate in His glory. Oh that the desire of seeking the face of God never cooled, but day by day grew more fervent ! There is, therefore, in the soul loving God an irrepressible desire of enjoying His sight, because the vision of God is the greatest happiness and most perfect felicity.

3. It therefore desires this blessedness; its entire longing is satisfied and set at rest by being joined to its end, because it can never be contented with any present good.

4. Besides, long experience has taught that by so much farther a person has strayed away from heavenly happiness, by so much the unhappier and more disturbed does he become, for in creatures

6—2

there is nothing lasting or durable, by which his affections can be assuaged. Return, therefore, to Him, by whom you have been made, and seek happiness from Him, from whom you had your beginning. For, indeed, He who created the soul is He who satisfies its desires in good things, and He has placed in the soul such an affection that when it is put aside there is no good by which it can be contented, there is no joy which it can securely possess.

5. Do not remain here, my soul, for it is not the place of your rest, but seek what is above, ascend to Him who made Thee : for He has sent you messengers, He invites you to ascend. With how many desires of eternal life has He inspired you ? how many messengers has He sent you ? at whose invitation prepare yourself to go to Him. Go if you desire to see Him, go if you endeavour to please Him, go if you renounce the things here below ; but whatever you do or omit, act from love.

6. For you, indeed, could not seek Him unless He had first sought you and moved you with holy desires towards Himself. The soul which is not enlightened and heated with the light of the eternal Sun languishes, not indeed with love, but with dangerous lukewarmness.

7. But if the soul shall be freed from tepidity and grief by the Spirit sweetly descending upon it, then it will soon burn with a desire of inspired light and of the secrets of the incomprehensible

Divinity. O immense force of the true Sun, which produces in the lover many ardent desires, dissipates the darkness of grief, makes labour light, and abundantly consoles the soul by one single visitation for many days and years of poverty ! O medicine of the soul, O bright light of the erring and wandering, shine always upon me, and prepare in me an abode till the perpetual light shine upon me !

8. When so many consolations flow from only a slight remembrance of Thee, how very sweet and pleasant will be Thy very presence ! I will freely turn myself to Thee, I will willingly renounce all things, that I may merit to be consoled by Thy grace.

9. It will not be difficult for a soul desirous of seeing Thy face to deprive itself of present pleasures, when it already feels interior consolation, or confidently expects soon to receive it from Thee.

10. Therefore let no one foolishly think that Thou wilt leave for any length of time a soul devoted to Thee without consolation, or that it shall receive small gifts for its many victories over nature ; because whatsoever be the earthly consolation, or from what source it comes, it cannot be compared to Thy heavenly consolation, either in quantity or quality of sweetness.

11. Study, therefore, O faithful soul, to so present yourself to Christ, your heavenly Spouse, that you may be always worthy of His grace and

consolation ; for you shall abundantly find in Him, and through Him, what will console you in every anxiety.

12. By so much the more frequently you approach Him, and the nearer you come to Him, by so much will He appear the more sweet and agreeable to you. But if you withdraw yourself from Him, you alone suffer loss, because He continues in His beauty and feels no grief or inconvenience.

13. You stand in need of His goodness : He does not require anything ; you can become happier by Him, but He does not by your proficiency ; He alone is sufficient for Himself, to Him alone nothing can be given, and from Him nothing can be taken away. All things that exist, live, feel, or understand, are so by His goodness ; justly, therefore, do all creatures bless and praise Him.

14. Oh that I were able to speak sufficiently of Him, and explain Him to you : you would then willingly praise Him. But what is unspeakable, as He is, cannot be explained, and what cannot be conceived cannot be thought of or expressed in words. As it is so, think, however, in the meantime and in a human way of your Creator, and bear in mind for your consolation His sweetness, till He shows you in His kingdom the presence of His countenance.

CHAPTER XIII

THE SIGHING OF A SOUL ON ACCOUNT OF THE DELAY OF GLORY

'I said in the excess of my mind, I am cast away from before Thy eyes.'—Ps. xxx.

1. My heart is smitten within me on account of the delay of Thy glory.   I will speak and converse in the bitterness of my soul.   The force of Thy love compels me to speak, and does not allow anything to be hidden from Thee.   What, therefore, shall I say ?   ' Behold, my God, in peace is my bitterness most bitter.'   He who does not understand knows not what these words mean.   It is not so with me, for I know and feel them.

2. I will speak to Thee, O Lord my God, to whom all things are known, and who didst give me knowledge and understanding in Thy good will, that I should not glory or be esteemed anything by the foolish.   There is no need to say this to Thee, as Thou knowest all things, and dost not expect consolation from others.   For what consolation could be given to Thee, who art the consolation of the desolate ?

3. Therefore everything may be useful to me, who am in need of the consolation of Thy words, that by good and sweet discourses I may excite my affections towards Thee, and prepare some refuge for my desolate soul.   For, as I cannot see

Thee present, I will grieve for Thee absent, because even this is a sign of love, and very sweet to the lover.

4. The meaning of this verse begins now to appear, for it is justly written of a loving soul. For by so much it ardently loves, and by so much it desires eternal goods, by so much does it truly feel in itself the truth of this verse. These are not cold words, unless to one who does not love.

5. Therefore the loving soul speaks to the Lord its God, and not to men, to whom it desires to be unknown. And if it sometimes speaks to men, it is but outwardly, that they may hear. Whatever it speaks to Thee, it speaks inwardly and by love more than by words.

6. 'Behold' (it says), 'in peace is my bitterness most bitter.' As it may be confessed, that when I found peace of mind by Thy goodness, the deceitful state of the world became more burthensome to me, for in this peace I see how far I was separated from the infinite good. And having been occupied by worldly desires and moved by various passions, I was very much hindered by interior troubles from the contemplation of heavenly things, for which I should anxiously sigh, but could not, because I had lost by negligence the feeling of interior sorrow.

7. But the tumult of vain thoughts being set aside, I begin to possess a little peace of heart, and am drawn by the whole desire of my soul to heavenly things; now I will weep more, that I

do not enjoy heavenly gifts, than I had before wept on account of being afflicted with the evils of the world. It is therefore bitterness to my soul to remain in this world, and to be oppressed with the burden of sin. But this becomes most bitter to me, who, to the best of my power, and with my affections directed to this end, now enjoy this happy peace, and am moved by my whole interior to embrace this eternal peace; yet, being detained in this mortal life, I cannot completely reach it.

8. I am therefore urged to cry to Thee with sighs, and to say, ' Unhappy man, who will free me from the body of this death ?' I do not feel a greater burden than to be exiled from Thee in this world, for, being absorbed in love, I require no consolation but Thee.

9. I have learned by most evident proof that my soul cannot be satisfied with any present good, or find true happiness, till it be received into the heavenly mansions and joined to Thee ; for though it may be wrapped in contemplation, burn with a desire of Thee, and love Thee exceedingly, yet its affections remain unsatisfied whilst in the body, and therefore its end is reached by the possession of Thee, the greatest good, and by the sight of Thy countenance.

10. O most amiable King of heaven, O my Beloved most beautiful and faithful, when wilt Thou fill me with the joy of Thy countenance ? when wilt Thou satisfy all my desires with Thy

continual happiness ? For my soul thirsts for Thee, and is very much afflicted in not finding Thee. So long as I live in the world and do not see Thee, everything that I behold is sorrowful to me.

11. In the meantime my heart is on fire, and in my ardour I say, not once, but often, 'When shall I come and appear before the face of the Lord ?' Love increases as time goes on, and desire becomes more ardent, so that I cease not to weep day and night, whilst I always think, where is my God ?

12. For it is sweet to the lover to weep for Thee when it cannot have what it desires, but must remain without Thee, and live in hope. The loving soul is more satisfied and comforted by these tears than if it had all earthly pleasures, for if it loved them it would by no means weep for Thee.

13. How holy and pleasing to Thee is the shedding of such tears, which indeed destroy all worldly joys and temporal pleasures, but obtain heavenly consolations. Therefore the shedding of holy tears is the gift only of the truly devout and loving.

14. There is another cause of tears to those who are surrounded with miseries : one weeps because he is very sick, another because he is oppressed, another because he suffers injuries, and another because he is opposed and contradicted, and each of these will sometimes weep.

15. I grieve, O my God, because it is not yet given me to enjoy Thee. I know whom I believe, and I am certain it is easier to deny that heaven and earth do not exist than that God is not. I know that He is truly the good of my soul, and that I never can be happy without the perfect contemplation of Him.

16. As the contemplation of Him without intermission is not yet given me to enjoy, I am very much grieved to be deprived of this great happiness, to be surrounded with the darkness of this life, and to be oppressed by my own infirmity, so that upon whatever I meditate of heavenly glory, I can but bring to it a light which is small and covered with a mist, and therefore do I often repeat with sighs that verse: 'And whilst each day it is said to me, Where is Thy God? my spirit is the more grieved.'

17. For I think in suspense, Where is my good? where is the perfect joy of my heart? where is my peace and rest? where are all the unspeakable goods unless in my God? And when shall I enjoy these, unless I am immediately joined to Him? And when will this be? Now I believe and hope, but do not possess Him. Where is my God whom I love, but do not see, whose love so often wounds me, whose absence affects me, and whose visitation often consoles me?

18. Where is my God, whom to have once seen is to have learned all things? Where is my God, in whom my heart and my flesh always desire to

exult ? Where is my God, for whom I bear so many labours and sorrows, whose sweet memory and dearer presence drive away all sadness from my heart ? Where is my hope, where is my glory ? Is it not in Thee, my God, the salvation of my countenance ?

19. Show me Thy glory, and do not turn away Thy face from me, and I will cease to complain. If I contend a little with myself, do not blame me, for ardent love has many wonderful ways. I am forced to await, but I am more moved to desire, and thus a friendly duel is continued in me.

CHAPTER XIV

THE REMEMBRANCE OF THE HEAVENLY COUNTRY

'Lord, I have loved the beauty of Thy house, and the place of the abode of Thy glory.'—Ps. xv.

1. LORD, Thou knowest well, and I cannot sufficiently express, how willingly I would be with Thee, and how fervently I desire it. I crave this, not only when evils are present, but even when great things are at hand ; my choice, however, is that I prefer to be with Thee. But how may my desire be satisfied ? It is disagreeable to me to be here, and it should be so ; I desire to be with Thee, and as yet it is not allowed.

2. I do not see otherwise than to bear the delay patiently, and to resign my will to Thee. What then ? Do I wish to murmur when this disposi-

tion is necessary? By no means. Many saints have indeed lived long in this world, whose hearts were, however, in heaven. If Thou wishest to prolong my exile. I will be submissive, so long as it will please Thee; nevertheless, as the desire of being with Thee may be more agreeable even in its expectation, I wish in the meantime to meditate with Thee upon the heavenly abode.

3. I do not, however, desire to pry into the smallest of the joys which Thou hast prepared for those who love Thee, but to meditate a little in general, that my affections, being often borne down and weakened by earthly affairs, may be again moved and raised up by the hope of eternal life.

4. O if that day would dawn, when the joys of heaven would receive me, how delighted would I then be, and how happy I would consider myself, secure in lasting peace! There would then be no need to investigate any more, when no secrets can be hidden; but my life is surrounded by night, and therefore it is no wonder if my eyes become darkened in the mist of Thy glory.

5. Still looking from afar, I will lift up my eyes and salute that holy city, Jerusalem, which is constructed above of living stones—that is, of angels and holy men. Come, come now, my soul, take to yourself the wings of desire and hasten upwards; leave your corporal senses, and depart from the visible figures of this world to the holy

abode of God, to the new Jerusalem, founded in
lasting peace, crowned with glory and honour,
and made perfect by the aggregation of every
good.

6. In it are wonderful and ineffable things, of
which it is not in man's power to speak. The
senses do not perceive, the human intellect
cannot conceive, how glorious is God in His
saints, and how wonderful in His majesty.
Extend thy thought to the highest heaven,
dilate thy desires to perpetual eternities, and
say with the prophet, ' Glorious things are said of
thee, O holy city of God.'

7. There whatever is desired is obtained, whatever is obtained is securely possessed. There
God is seen face to face, clearly and without any
obscurity, not passing or for a short time, but
fixedly and without end. There is known the
blessed and glorious Trinity and the inseparable
Unity, who is adored, praised, and blessed by all
the citizens of heaven.

8. There is He, my Lord Jesus Christ, the only
and singly Beloved, more precious than all goods,
my longed-for treasure, the immortal Spouse of
the Church, in whom are all the treasures of the
wisdom and knowledge of God, hidden from the
world but manifested to His blessed. Oh, how
joyful are all the saints before the face of the
Holy of Holies, the cause and source of their
salvation! For there He does not speak in proverbs, but He tells them plainly of the Father.

9. He is their book, the Word with the Father in the beginning, teaching all things and filling all so that no glory is absent from them. O happy and everlasting glory, which is not of passing memory, but of the presence of God in the splendour of His saints.

10. There is the most glorious mother of God, Mary ever Virgin, adorning the whole court of heaven with her grace and beauty, surrounded and accompanied by multitudes of virgins, as the flowers of roses and the lilies of the valleys. There are angels and archangels; there are patriarchs and prophets; there are the heralds of Christ, the Apostles and disciples of our Lord, illustrious, and worthy of every veneration; there are the gorious maityrs purpled in their blood; there are the illustrious confessors, who, despising the world, merited to become citizens of heaven; there are the young men and virgins, the old with the young continually praising the name of God, ascribing to the Divine Majesty whatever of good or virtue they ever did, always grateful, always devoted, always joyful, always inflamed with love, never oppressed with weariness, but intent in the continual contemplation of God.

11. Oh, how glorious is the kingdom in which all the saints reign with Christ, clothed with the richest garments, and secure from every evil! There they follow the Lamb wherever He goes, for there shall be no separation from Him, but full of joy they will for ever rejoice in God.

12. O my soul, contemplate these things, and withdraw thy thoughts from all that is visible. Indeed, this place is holy, and the Lord is in it. Here peace and joy always abound; here is an overflowing of every good; here is the perpetual absence of every evil.

13. Oh, if you could conceive, even a little, the ineffable joys of the saints, from which your pilgrimage could draw some consolation; for here you shall find but labours and sorrows, the assaults of temptation, and conflict with the world. Oh, if the Author of heavenly light would deign to inspire you a little, and would not leave you empty with my insipid food, but, according to the riches of His superabundant grace, would empty and purify you from all material things, and lead you soon to the immensity of his eternal brightness! Give me, O Lord God, to know and understand the perfect happiness of the saints, not from books, but by the Holy Spirit, who teaches heavenly secrets more than the human mind can conceive. Grant that my life be much more fervent and spiritual, and in the midst of great trials to hold bravely the palm of patience, till, having paid the debt of Nature, I may, in Thy mercy, reach that happiness which I desire.

END OF BOOK II

BOOK III

THE MISERIES WHICH THE GOOD ENDURE IN THIS WORLD

CHAPTER I

THE DEVOUT ARE TRIED BY CONTRARY THINGS

' Rejoice, ye just, in the Lord.'—Ps. xxxii.

1. IN heaven there is always joy, in hell always sadness ; in the world both are for a time, in order to prove the good and bad. By stripes the soul is humbled and purified, pride is confounded, and vainglory disappears.

2. So long as the soul abides in the body, it is exercised in both, for greater proficiency in the love of Christ. It is therefore a great art, it is a great virtue, to use well both good and bad things.

3. Bless, therefore, O my soul, the Lord at all times ! Praise, O Sion, thy God day and night, and great will be thy reward everywhere before God, both in heaven and on earth. All things, prosperous and adverse, good and bad, joyful and sad, will be useful to thee. Hence the Apostle St. Paul said, ' To those who love God, all things co-

operate to their good.' Again, 'Nothing is wanting to those who fear Him.' Blessed are they who in all things follow the will of God.

CHAPTER II

THE ELECT ARE PROVED IN MANY WAYS

'It is written by the prophet, 'The patience of the poor shall not perish in the end.'—Ps. ix.

1. Great, O Lord my God, is the patience of Thy servants, and this is the victory of those who overcome all adversities in this world. For Thou hast said, ' In your patience you shall possess your souls.' Thou provest us in many ways, and Thou surroundest us on every side with tribulations, now external, now internal ; now Thou triest us with open temptations, and then with hidden ones, so that our whole being passes through the fire of temptation.

2. It is Thy will that we be tempted in all and tried in many things, that, having been proved in all and delivered from many miseries, we may return great thanks to Thy mercy and goodness. This seems pleasing and good in Thy sight, and is conducive to our proficiency. If Thou, O Lord our God, be for us, who can prevail against us ?

3. I will follow Thee, O Lord, whithersoever Thou goest, provided Thou art my guide in the way. If I shall walk in the midst of the shadows of death, I will fear no evil, for Thou art with me.

However, I will confess to the Lord my injustice against myself, and I will not hide my infirmity, if, perchance, I shall receive from my good Physician the balm of consolation. Behold, O Lord, my poverty and infirmity ; attend to what I say, for I have revealed to Thee my state. Now I desire rest, but Thou enjoinest labour ; I aspire after great things, but Thou proposest humble ones ; I seek an abundance of pleasure, but Thou persuadest the hardship of poverty.

4. I beseech Thee, O Lord, to let that be done, as Thou hast said. Thou who hast given the counsel, give also the help. Let all that which appears bitter to the flesh be made sweet ; let the burden that had seemed unbearable be made light. Let my flesh exult in the living God, and my spirit in God my Saviour. O Israel, how good is God to those who are of an upright spirit !

5. I love Thee, O Lord my strength, my support, my refuge, and, following in Thy footsteps and in those of Thy saints, I will now prefer poverty to riches, humility to glory, and patience to rest.

6. I will have care of these things, and whatever the spirit requires will be pleasing to me ; for the flesh profits nothing. May I be delighted with these, as with all riches, and let not the feet of the proud rich and of those living in pleasure move me. But I will rejoice in my Lord and exult in God my Jesus, who became for me an example of poverty, humility, and obedience.

CHAPTER III

GOD IS TO BE PRAISED IN THE ABSENCE OF DEVOTION

'The poor and needy shall praise Thy name, O Lord.'—
Ps. xlvii.

1. WHEN you feel dry, cold, and sad in prayer
and in meditation on the things of God, you should
not therefore despair or discontinue to humbly call
on Jesus, but should in the poverty of your spirit
praise God and give Him thanks; you should
willingly read for your consolation this verse:
'The poor and needy shall praise Thy name, O
Lord.'

2. Many saints and devout people were sometimes without consolation and left by God, that
they might learn patience and compassion for
others by their own experience of poverty and
grief, and also that they might not presume too
much on themselves in the time of devotion and
gladness.

3. Read also with the prophet the following
verse in the Psalms: 'But I indeed am needy and
poor, but the Lord is solicitous of me.' In the
Lord I will trust, because He is my strength and
salvation, which is true, for every good is from
God. Do not therefore presume, when you are
joyful, and do not be dejected when you are
burdened with grief; but be content in all things
which are pleasing in the sight of God: for you

have nothing good of yourself, but all goodness is from God.

4. When the grace of devotion is given, the sun from heaven shines upon you, the soul is enlightened, and exults as in riches ; but you foolishly deceive yourself if you presume and are puffed up. But when grace is secretly taken away and withdrawn from the ungrateful, then indeed you are poor and weak, unable to bear anything, and to pray is troublesome.

5. Accept as a benefit from God that He makes you poor, and humbles you with His elect, and chastises you with the rod for His children in punishment of your hidden excesses and many daily negligences, in order that you despise and think lowly of yourself, as St. Paul advises in his Epistle to the Romans, ' Be not wise, but fear.' It is great profit to the soul to think vilely of itself, and ascribe entirely to God every good.

CHAPTER IV

THE TRUE LOVER OF GOD

' Love the Lord, all ye His saints.'—Ps. xxx.

1. THE true lover of God loves Him purely—that is, he loves God for God, and to enjoy Him alone ; He loves Him not for any personal convenience, comfort, or reward coming from it, but entirely and finally on account of His infinite goodness and most excellent majesty. Therefore the

Psalmist often tells us 'to confess to the Lord, for He is good'; and this saying is sweet to the lover.

2. But the Psalmist, moreover, says, 'for His mercy is unto eternity'; these words are most consoling to the penitent and contrite. Therefore, O man, prone to evil, do not despair, as it is added, 'for His mercy is unto eternity.' He who humbles himself most profoundly and loves God most ardently is very pleasing to Him.

3. Blessed is he who considers himself viler than all, and avoids what he knows is displeasing to God. Blessed is he who for God and His good pleasure does every work from charity, with a pure intention, and refers his every thought entirely to the honour, praise, and glory of God. Blessed is he who retains nothing for himself, but freely returns to God all that he has received from Him.

CHAPTER V

THE SOUL SHOULD BE GRATEFUL FOR EVERY GIFT

'Magnify the Lord with me, and let us extol His name together.'— Ps. xxxiii.

1. HE who gives the greatest thanks for even the smallest gifts very much praises God, because He who gives them is supreme over all.

2. Nothing which the Most High freely and gratuitously gives should appear small or vile. God requires nothing more than that He be gratefully loved, that every offence be avoided, and that

gratitude be always and everywhere rendered to Him. He is great before God who despises himself, places himself below others, considers himself unworthy of all graces and benefits, does not foolishly exalt himself on account of any good, and does not desire the praises of others.

3. But he is greater who, like Job, gives thanks, rejoices, and blesses God, when he is stricken, despised, reproached, made poor, neglected, tempted, afflicted, scorned, and put to confusion; who reckons all hardships and difficulties befalling him as great benefits which he bears for God, and does not complain, but gives thanks, rejoices, and blesses God.

4. Blessed is he who, like Job, piously receives from the hand of God the stroke of affliction, and entirely offers and commits himself to the Divine Will. Blessed is he who always seeks and chooses what is most pleasing to God, who accepts disagreeable things as pleasing, who being injured is joyful, and who esteems temporal loss as spiritual gain.

CHAPTER VI

THE CONFORMITY OF A DEVOUT SOUL WITH ITS CRUCIFIED LORD

' I am with him in tribulation.'—Ps. xc.

1. WHAT is this, O Lord? Explain the word which Thou hast spoken; lay open the sense of this verse for the comfort of Thy servant.

2. Hear, O son, when you are in trouble and grief of heart, then you are with Jesus upon the cross ; and when you are consoled in devotion and rejoice in hymns and Divine canticles, then you arise with Jesus in newness of spirit, and, as it were, come forth from the sepulchre of sin, singing joyfully, Alleluia !

3. But when you pray on bended knees for your sins, feel internal sorrow and supplicate for them, then you knock violently at the gate of heaven. But when you neglect all earthly things, and meditate only on heavenly, then you ascend with Jesus to heaven, and are associated with the angels.

4. Be therefore meek, humble, and penitent, for God's sake, on every occasion and in every trial that befalls you, and carry your cross patiently with Jesus, because every affliction of the flesh patiently borne is a medicine for the soul, a satisfaction for sins, and a hope of future happiness and glory.

CHAPTER VII

GOD IS THE HELPER AND REFUGE OF THE POOR

'To Thee the poor is left. Thou wilt be a helper to the orphan.'—Ps. x.

1. BLESSED is the poor who has God for his helper in every tribulation, his comfort in every anguish, his only hope and confidence in difficulties, and

his crown of glory in the kingdom of eternal happiness. Voluntary poverty is a precious virtue practised by Christ, the eternal reward of which is with the angels in heaven, where neither the thief can enter to steal it nor the robber to kill the possessor of it.

2. The rich of this world are surrounded with many dangers and daily anxieties from which the servant of Christ is free, by the renunciation of all things that are in the world. Great is the freedom of a faithful soul that has no property in anything on account of the kingdom of God and the love of Jesus Christ, but possesses all in Christ, who became poor and afflicted for us—who, had not where to rest His head, and who, hanging naked upon the cross, could not move His hands or feet.

3. Who is like to Him, poor in all His sufferings? Truly, no one. On account of this, the name of Him alone is exalted above all things in heaven and on earth, and blessed above all for eternity. O good poverty, unless God had first assumed thee, thy severity would now be despised by all! Blessed poverty of goods, which takes away the pride of eyes and the occasion of many sins!

4. He is truly poor in spirit who does not take pride in any word or act, and who does not desire to be in a higher place, lest he should grievously fall. Oh, great is the virtue of poverty, which renounces all, has nothing of its own, opens the

gate of heaven to the soul, increases the crown of glory, and after the anguish of this life, spent in the service of Christ, merits to receive the palm of patience with the martyrs.

5. To bear want and many inconveniences for the love of Christ is truly and really to serve Him. Blessed is he who makes a virtue of his wants and infirmities, and is submissive to the will of God in everything he suffers. Do not therefore, O poor, be too much troubled when you are in want, or indignant when you are despised and abandoned by your friends.

6. Turn your heart to Christ, who became poor and afflicted for you; seek thy comfort from God, and from Him alone, if you desire to be always joyful; for all other consolation sought outside God is nothing, passing and insufficient, though it may appear great. Choose, therefore, Jesus Christ, the Son of God, for your special and intimate Friend, and leave all others for Him. Beware of every companion who would hinder you from serving Christ, and draw you to the world and to the gates of hell.

7. He alone who can give the kingdom of heaven to all renouncing the world and its vanities is sufficient to give perfect comfort; for the world and its concupiscence pass by like a puff of wind, or like the flower of the field that withers away. Stand, therefore, most firm in your good resolution of always serving God and of keeping the vows of your baptism, at which you offered yourself

entirely to Him, that you may rejoice exceedingly in the kingdom of Christ with His saints.

8. Eternal rest in heaven will be given you for little labour and passing sorrow in this world. Think seriously again and again on the sacred wounds of Christ and on the painful sores of Lazarus, which will be useful to you in your agony at death and passage from the world.

CHAPTER VIII

LAZARUS POOR AND INFIRM

' I am poor and sorrowful, O God, help me.'—Ps. lxviii.

1. THIS is the voice of the poor and infirm sighing to God for his kingdom. O poor and infirm man, bear patiently for a short time the pains of body and the want of food and clothes, for you shall not be long here to suffer. Give thanks to God, for it is better to be chastised now with the poor and weak than to be tortured hereafter with the great and rich.

2. Remember your past sins, by which you offended God and your neighbour; bear the chastisement of the Lord for their remission, for which you have neither sincerely repented nor fully satisfied. Remember also, for your consolation, all the great sorrows and sacred wounds of Christ; for He bore for you more and greater sufferings. Bear in mind also, for your encouragement, that Lazarus, poor and covered with sores,

was joyfully received into Abraham's bosom;
and fear the end of the pampered rich man, who,
after all his feasting, was buried in hell, from
which he shall never be delivered.

3. See now which is better for you to choose—
whether to suffer a little now, to be in want with
the infirm Lazarus, and to be for ever happy with
Christ; or to have, with the rich glutton, abundance of pleasure for a short time, to die suddenly,
to be buried in hell, and to burn for ever with the
devils. These few words are sufficient for the
intelligent. Blessed is he who understands, and
in good time corrects himself of his evil ways,
that he may not be damned with the wicked and
tortured with great punishments. For those
whom holy words do not now affect or correct
shall afterwards be torn without profit, with
cruel stripes, and shall be tortured without intermission.

4. From these evils poor and infirm Lazarus
was freed, and joyfully carried by holy angels
into Abraham's bosom. Hear, moreover, the
many benefits of God mercifully given to this poor
Lazarus. He had not (as I think) rich friends to
visit him, or any servants or companions to attend
him; but (as Jesus says) dogs came and licked
his sores. He had these only for comfort in his
misery; and what is more miserable than a man
to be destitute of human comfort, and to be left
to beasts for it? And yet a word of impatience
or murmur does not come from the mouth of this

afflicted man, but, on the contrary, thanksgiving and praise.

5. You, therefore, O weak man, do not murmur if you are left for awhile without consolation, and if you feel the pains of infirmity, but consider that these come to you by the dispensation of Divine providence, that being afflicted and chastised here, you may not perish hereafter. He perhaps fell into very small faults, but you have been guilty of very great sins. Therefore bear patiently the pains of infirmity, and rejoice that you are sometimes abandoned by men, that you may merit with Lazarus to enter the gate of the kingdom of heaven.

CHAPTER IX

THE UNION OF THE SOUL WITH GOD IN THE VARIOUS CRISES OF LIFE

1. Who will console you, if God Himself be not your Comforter ? and who will more kindly bear your infirmities but He who carries all without burden ? and if you feel sad, to whom will you more safely reveal it than to Him who knows all ? and in whom will you have greater faith than in Him who never fails in truth ?

2. Hear, ye children of earth and sons of men, it is possible and very easy for God to do what is written, ' both rich and poor together.' I am poor and in want of all things. My God is rich, and does not need anything. My Beloved to me

(he says) and I to Him, who feedeth among the lilies. This is the testimony of the spouses. The second is like to this : ' I will, O Father, that all be one, as we are one.'

3. If you wonder at the greatness of this union, be silent and admire the excellence of His goodness, and also the wonderful union in the assumption of our humanity. It is right for Him to do what He wills, who alone does wonderful things, and if you seek the reason, you will find it in the goodness of His will.

4. Oh sweet companionship with Christ and under the protection of Christ ! O gracious union, full of love and sweetness of the Holy Ghost, which can be more easily felt than described ! These graces belong to the soul that has made itself a stranger to all worldly affairs—to a soul not held by the love of the present life, and that bears the secret of its mind heavenwards.

CHAPTER X

THE BELOVED GIVING THE REASON OF HIS WITH- DRAWING

1. THE voice of the Beloved sounded and said : ' I am He who speaks justice.' Who is like Me in counsel and prudence ? Who made the sea and dry land ? I, the Lord, forming light and creating darkness. Who entered the abyss, and drew waters from the depth ? I, the Lord, searching

the hearts and reins. Who knew all that is new and old ? I, the Lord, who made all things in number, weight, and measure. I am the Creator of heaven and earth, and the Ruler of all ages.

2. I am the knower of secrets and the revealer of hidden things ; I embrace the universe, and see the causes of each thing. I am God, and am not changed, with whom the reasons of changeable things remain unchanged. I am the omnipotent God, whose power is supreme ; I am the Most High, whose height cannot be reached ; I am Goodness, whose being cannot be conceived.

3. I am most present and yet most secret ; I am the nearest and the most remote to the senses ; I bear all without burden ; I rule all without discussion ; I behold the past as well as the future, as I do also the present ; I am beyond all corporal as well as spiritual creation ; I am named in many ways, but not truly conformable to any knowledge.

4. I suddenly appear, and immediately without perception I disappear. I am truly a hidden God, who dispenses in a thousand ways My gifts to those who love Me. I have said these things even to the loving soul. I will hide My face from it for a little while, and I will leave it for a moment, to see if it truly loves Me. It is a good thing to love purely—that is, to love Me, not on account of yourself, nor of any temporal convenience, nor of spiritual consolation, but to love Me solely for

Myself, and to finally love yourself on My account, and to expect nothing for your love.

5. All do not so love Me, but only the most perfect souls have these qualities of chaste love. But the love that is yet imperfect requires to be often exercised and proved, that it may know how great it is, and through it reach a contempt of one's self.

6. You have said in your heart, indeed I love, and you often repeat the same thing, because you love; but I do not believe merely your words and thoughts, for I will prove you in truth. When I am present and caress you, when I give devotion, or increase it, when I bestow not only what is profitable, but also pleasant, then you piously say, ' My Beloved, I love Thee '; and you say well, for I am exceedingly lovable, and everything that can be said or thought of Me is always amiable, sweet, and praiseworthy.

7. But what great thing is it to love and praise Me only for My gifts? Sinners do this; indeed, they often bless Me when they receive what they had inordinately desired. Praise in the mouth of a sinner is not acceptable. Who, therefore, loves Me for My gifts and consolations does no more than the avaricious. Advance, advance, and ascend to what is more perfect.

8. It is always disagreeable to be weak and delicate; learn to live on solid food, and be no longer nourished with the milk of little ones. Pass on to the number of the brave Davids

having the spear, sword, and helmet ; take up the cross and follow Me ; hasten to be numbered among those who know how to bear for Me divers difficulties and troubles in this land of exile.

9. You are too much inclined to consolation ; I wish, therefore, to prove you and to draw you to the other side, that you may experience what you can suffer, and may not appear to yourself innocent and holy. I will send to you tribulation, anger, indignation, and temptations by the wicked.

10. Some will take what is yours, others will deny you what you want ; some will detract you, others will reproach you ; some will place a great burden upon you, others will send you where you do not like ; some will afflict you internally, others externally ; some shall be raised to places and honours, and you shall be left to contempt and labours.

11. In all these and in greater you shall be proved as a brave athlete. I will not depart from you or let you go till I have diligently examined you, if you will bless Me to My face. But if you love Me with your whole heart, and bless My name at all times, it is just that from hence you should be interiorly filled with greater grace.

12. But if you are not yet able to bear My rod, and think My discipline less lovable, grieving often for My presence, which you affectionately

8

and earnestly ask, I will send you help to arise, and I will come, and you shall be restored to your former grace. I do not wish that you be entirely dejected, for I love those loving Me. And if you do not as yet love Me perfectly, I do not, however, despise you, but I will take care that you increase in love. I have care of you that you do well, and I do not wish that you should doubt of Me.

13. I know well what you are able to bear, and I therefore temper My visitations, lest you should be tempted more than you are able to bear, and fall away. But if I delay, expect Me even to the day of visitation. Coming, I will come, and will fulfil My promises. You, however, be intent in prayer, apply yourself to holy reading, be patient and long-suffering in all things.

14. I am not ignorant that you are sometimes in grief, that you are soon dejected and give up all hope, as if I were not to return; this is by no means pleasing to Me. Where is your faith? You have need of great faith, especially in this matter, for if you do not see Me, you are, however, seen by Me, to whom you should commit yourself in all things. For though you are ignorant of My judgments, a lively faith tells you that whatever God disposes and does is good.

15. I, therefore, console you, because this infirmity will not be to death, but for the glory of God. I have taken away your desire, and I wish to try your faith and love. I have done

all these things that you may better know your infirmity, and better understand My goodness. You do not know yourself as well as I know you ; I know you and all things concerning you, not only in time, but from eternity.

16. Know, therefore, what may come to you from Me. See how poor you are of yourself if, perchance, you are left by Me. You have not yet made much proficiency in the knowledge of yourself, and, as it is very expedient that you should know this, I wish you to learn it from experience. It is good for you to be sometimes desolate, afflicted, and humbled, so that you may more keenly feel your infirmity.

17. I know that this conduces very much to your proficiency if from it you become more prudent and faithful in your actions. What have you lost ? You are deceived by self-love, and when you do not think of the giver you abuse the gift. I have filled you, but you have forgotten ; you are as a bunch of grapes from the vine.

18. Examine now yourself, see what strength you have, and if it be from yourself why have you not kept it ? But as you have not been able to keep it, know that you have received it from above. Give, therefore, honour to grace, and confess that you can do nothing without Me. Consider how necessary I am to you, how sufficient and alone able to confirm you in every good. Where were you before I called you,

8—2

unless in your sins ?   But now you run in the way of My commandments, because I have loosened your bonds and led you into this way.

CHAPTER XI

THE SAME SUBJECT CONTINUED

1. *Soul :* Thou alone, O Lord, art my one and most excellent Beloved, most faithful in all and above all.

2. *Lord :* Why, therefore, did you foolishly think with yourself to follow other lovers ? What did you find displeasing in Me ?   Was it My glory or beauty ?

3. *Soul :* Indeed, O Lord, there is none like Thee in beauty and glory, in riches and power, nor is there such in heaven or on earth.   For Thou alone art most high above every creature. Thine are the heavens, Thine is the earth; Thou hast established the universe in its beauty.

4. Thou hast given very much to creatures, in whom are reflected Thy great beauty, wisdom, and goodness ; but nothing in comparison to Thy blessed and glorious presence. Now I have learned from experience how bitter it is to have left Thee even for an hour.

5. *Lord :* Return, therefore, to Me, says the Beloved.   It is enough that you have until now wandered about.   Be now steady and meek, hoping and trusting in Me, not only in the day of

visitation, but more so in the night of temptation. I have left you so that, being soon fatigued, you would quickly return, and, being disappointed with exterior consolation, you would at length understand what My love, which so often invited you, bestowed on you.

6. Now, therefore, bear in mind (and not without reason) that you are sometimes left to yourself, that you have no sensible devotion, that you feel disgust, that you are tried with temptation, that you are afflicted on every side, that you do not find counsel, that you receive no help, and that from every quarter you suffer anguish and desolation. Therefore do I leave you, that you may know how necessary is My presence for you, not only in one thing or in a great event, but in every act, in every place, and at every time, as well in the morning as in the evening, and wheresoever you are, or whithersoever you go, or wherever you rest.

7. I leave you, that you may know how much you love Me, and may see the measure of your love. You imagine yourself stronger and happier than you are ; but it is quite evident that when I withdraw from you a little you are poor and miserable. How will your love be known, unless by bearing meekly the difficulties of life ?

8. Sometimes I see you tepid, and in order to excite you to fervour and to diligence in seeking Me, I hide Myself from you for a time, as the Beloved behind the partition. I see and know

all. Trials are useful for many things: they often give great intelligence. Even if you love Me, do not delay to seek Me. If I am pleasing, take care to find Me with diligence.

9. Are you ignorant that riches acquired by labour are kept more carefully? By whom is rest more required than by the fatigued? To whom is love more pleasant than to him who felt sorrow for the Beloved? A treasure which was lost, but found, is twice dearer than it was before. I therefore usefully withdraw myself, and I do so, not in displeasure, but with a certain pious dispensation I so act with My beloved. But I give permission to return to Me as often as you feel need. I never close My ears to one who humbly and fervently prays to Me.

CHAPTER XII

PRAISE OF RELIGIOUS POVERTY

1. WOULD that holy poverty were deeply imprinted on your heart. I have heard your sighs, how you are distressed, and this has been displeasing to Me. Is it not this that I chose? Arise, and go over to Bethlehem with the shepherds, and see the Word made flesh, and know that poverty was not absent from it.

2. See My poverty, and in comparison to it your poverty will be very little. For I being rich and not in need of anything, I was not ashamed to

become poor and an exile in this world, and this for you.   But you, who are poor and naked, who brought nothing into the world, should you not consider this ?   Let your complaining now cease. You should not now banquet and rejoice, but in future.

3. The servants of God should not rejoice in present things, or conform themselves to the pomps of the world, but, having despised its pleasures, should embrace the delights of poverty. Indeed, my poverty and humility are pleasing to the hearts of those who despise worldly riches.

4. Perhaps you wish to be clothed in purple and fine linen, and to dine sumptuously ; take care that it do not happen to you to be for ever tortured with the rich man in hell ; for this is My judgment, because their works follow them.   Now, one thing follows, that you bear want patiently, or you shall not be in the number of My poor.

5. I have pointed out the beautiful way to the poor ; I have opened the door to those who labour and knock ; I have thrown open the gates of My kingdom to the humble, and the rich shall not pass through them.   Do you wish to know who shall enter ?   Open your eyes and see : ' But it happened that the beggar died, and was carried by angels into Abraham's bosom.'

Servant : And who is he who may be able to follow him ?

6. *Lord :* Remember, son, that this Lazarus was covered with sores and full of misery, who in

hunger and thirst sat before the gates of the rich man ; and he, who bore so much for My name, was he not worthy to enter into My joy ?   Imitate him, if you will, for his soul was pleasing to Me ; and whence was it pleasing ?   Because his poverty and patience first pleased Me.   Go you and do likewise.

7. Amen, I say to you, unless you be converted and become as this Lazarus, or as one of My poor, you shall not be received by the angels into heaven.   No one shall enter unless he is clean, and if he be not clean, My Father will purify him in the fire of poverty, and will cleanse him in the water of temptation ; and being thus made clean, he shall return after death to the company of the saints.   Have you understood all these things ?

Servant : Yes, Lord.

8. *Lord :* And now, what shall I say ?   The hour comes, and it is now, that many shall not receive this wholesome doctrine, but each one will indulge rather in that which seems pleasing and delightful to him.   But you have not so learned Jesus Christ, before whose eyes poverty was always present.   Far different did that saint think who said, ' Thou hast prepared in my sight a table against those who afflict me '; ' Thou hast prepared in Thy sweetness for the poor, O Lord.' And again, he joyfully sings, ' For I am needy and poor,' and, ' The poor and needy will praise Thy name.'   O poverty, my friend, he who despises

you despises Me, and he who receives you receives Me. I know you are not loved by all; I am silent when you are sometimes rejected with indignation. They have done all these things to you because they have not known you, and of what merit you are with Me. You, however, fear not, for I am He who chose you; I purchased you; I esteemed you more precious than all riches, and sweeter than all delights; I sought from infancy, and I have never departed from you.

CHAPTER XIII

THE COMMENDATION OF POVERTY FROM THE EXAMPLE OF CHRIST AND HIS SAINTS

1. O ALL you who pass by the way, attend and see, is there such poverty as My poverty? Daughters of Sion, come now together, and see King Solomon in the crown with which His mother crowned him—how she laid in a manger Him who always possessed the power of His Father; how she folded in garments Him who holds in His hands heaven and earth.

2. Poverty should be loved, but it appears to the rich foolishness and to the proud ignominy, but to Me and My elect wisdom and glory.

3. Men truly poor rejoice in the Holy Ghost, and say, 'As, having nothing and possessing all things, as poor and enriching many, considering all things as dung that they may gain Christ. I

say to you, poor, hear Me, for you are of My sheep.
Do not fear, little flock, for it pleased My Father
to give you a kingdom. You lead here a poor life
indeed, but you shall have many goods, if you
love poverty. If you will love Me, you shall
indeed rejoice, for I came into the world to
evangelize the poor.

4. When I was in the world I loved poverty,
but I refused to have riches, because they are not
from the Father, but they are of the world. For
those who wish to become rich in this world fall
into the snares of the devil, and into various
desires of the heart, and it is difficult for them to
enter into the kingdom of heaven.

5. But My kingdom is not of this world; if it
was of this world, My servants indeed would
attend Me, and be present with Me in great
numbers; but My kingdom is not here, and I
became the servant and minister of the whole
world. For I did not come to be served, but to
serve, and to give My life for the redemption of
many. Therefore, O my poor, incline your ears
to the words of My mouth, and learn from Me,
that I have led the way for you in poverty.

6. Let your poverty be sufficient for you, and
esteem it as riches. Be glad and rejoice with it,
for your reward is very great in heaven. Let not
your heart be disturbed, and do not fear, for I am
He who speaks to you. Be not sad or troubled
because you have not riches, but rejoice in the
Lord your God because you have despised them,

and are become the poor of Christ. O holy and praiseworthy poverty, how shall I extol you, how shall I proclaim you, how shall I recommend you to my friends? Oh, what a wonderful example I have shown to all who are poor for Me, who became poor for them!

CHAPTER XIV

THE CONNECTION AND RELATIONSHIP OF POVERTY WITH HUMILITY

1. THAT poverty which is a stranger to humility is not to be praised, nor is that humility which despises poverty pleasing to God. It is a sign of hidden pride to be ashamed of poor clothes, and to glory in them is the vice of hypocrisy. Humility is not ashamed to walk in old sandals, because many of the saints passed their lives in bare feet.

2. It is read of the prophet Isaias that the Lord said to him, ' Go and divest thyself of the covering of thy loins, and take the sandals from thy feet'; and he did so, and went naked and barefooted. Behold a strong evidence to prove this truth! The table of poverty is content with simple food, which only is necessary, and humility most willingly consents to be present for My name at this refection of sobriety.

3. I know how to abound and to suffer want; I can do all things in Him who comforts me.

Poverty knows how to accommodate itself compassionately to the infirm and weak, but it proposes hard things to the great, who would always have that by which they may become richer. It often insists on labour and fatigue, nor does it eat its bread in idleness, that it may fulfil the words of the Apostle, who says, 'I was burdensome to no one, but in labour day and night, I did not eat my bread in idleness.'

4. Humility working together with poverty complains of some by the prophet, ' For they are not in the labours of men, and with men they do not receive stripes, therefore does pride possess them.' And in the Gospel, when the Lord saw some standing idle in the market-place, He rebuked them, saying, ' Why do you stand idle all the day ? Go you also into My vineyard, and what is just I will give you.'

5. Poverty takes rest in poor beds, or sometimes upon straw or mattress or ground, whatever it may be. Humility does not rest upon soft or costly beds, and is resolved not to have the smallest friendship with any of the things of the world.

6. It is read that John was covered with camel's hair, and they who are clothed in soft garments are in the palaces of kings ; and it was heard of Me that the foxes have their dens, and the birds their nests, but the Son of man has not where to lay His head. Poverty does not possess men or women servants, riches or palaces, or any

of those things which contribute to the comfort or convenience of the present life.

7. Humility has not, and does not desire to have, those things ; but it wishes to be like the Son of God, and says, ' I came to serve, not to be served ; I am the handmaid of Christ, and it is not becoming to me to rule.   I have resolved to serve only the Creator of all things, and how could I for a moment attend to the vain and passing things of this world ?   Let everything which does not savour of poverty be far from me and from my house.

CHAPTER XV

THE CONSOLATION OF POVERTY

1. I AM, said the Lord God, the Father of the poor and Judge of the orphans and widows ; I have heard the desire of the poor, and My ear was attentive to their cry and needs.   Do not touch them, and do not hurt them either by force or by fraud, for I am the Avenger of all.   Do not desire to trouble them, for all the poor are Mine.

2. And now where are My poor ?   Have you not heard My voice ?   Behold, how many proofs I have given that My friend poverty would be delightful and agreeable to you.   I have called it friend, that all the kings and princes of the earth may learn not to despise it, but to receive and honour it as the very dearest which the King of

heaven and earth, who is above all kings, dedicated in His sacred infancy. If you do not believe My words, believe at least My works. Go therefore and see the place where the Lord was placed, either in the manger or in the sepulchre. Am I not the Christ? Feel therefore and see that I had not riches or pleasures, but poor garments and a winding-sheet. Believe now that I was not rich, and that I loved poverty. These should be sufficient in praise of poverty, which is truly laudable and should be loved by all the servants of God, because He and all His saints preferred it to all riches.

CHAPTER XVI

THE NECESSITY OF PATIENCE IN THE MIDST OF THE MISERIES OF LIFE

1. WHAT is my life but a prolonged misery from the day of my birth to that of my death? and there is no rest between them, but a multiplicity of labours and sorrows. And, O my God, how have I come into this misery? Thou knowest well how many miseries surround me, placed in the prison of my body, and there is no one who knows so well the miseries of men as Thou knowest, O Lord our God. See therefore how necessary for me is patience.

2 Why is it, my soul, that thou art in the land of enemies? For if thou hadst walked in the way of the Lord, thou shouldst indeed have peace

on the earth.   Thou hast left the Lord your God,
the fountain of living water, and hast dug for
yourself cisterns which cannot hold water, and
therefore thou art delivered into the hands of
thy enemies.

3. But return to Me, said the Lord, and I will
receive you.   On account of my sins, O Lord, all
these things came upon me by Thy just judgment.
I have sinned with my fathers, and I carry the
heavy burden placed upon all the sons of Adam,
for all his sons are sons of wrath.

4. But unless Thou hadst given us help from
heaven, we had been as Sodom and like Gomorra,
which were destroyed in a moment.   Therefore
Thy mercies are great, O Lord, that we have not
been consumed, and Thy goodness is very great
that we are yet living.   We are all sons of death,
but Thou didst go before us in Thy miseries, and
Thy judgment was not as our sins, for Thy mercy
was greater than all our wicked works.

5. Remember, we are dust, and man is as grass
and as the flower of the field ; but I know Thy
right judgment is the cause of all miseries.   However, I yet desire to know from all these what may
be the consolation in Christ Jesus our Lord.
And if I do not deserve to be fully consoled, give
me at least a little consolation.   Who will then
console my soul ?   I have found many deceivers,
narrating to me sinful fables, but not Thy law,
O Lord.

6. O best Comforter, sweet Guest of my soul,

my safe refuge, who fills every creature with blessing, open Thy hands, and bestow a blessing from heaven upon my parched land. I stretch out my hands to Thee, for I am as earth without water. Quickly hear me, O Lord, for my spirit fails me. And whither shall I go without Thee ? and to whom shall I flee ? Thou art the Lord my God, and therefore graciously receive my prayer.

7. I have raised up my soul to Thee, do not Thou despise me ; I have shown Thee my misery, do not turn away Thy eyes from me ; I have sinned, do not condemn me. My heart spoke to Thee, and my face sought Thee ; O Lord, do not abandon me. But Thyself hast said, wishing to console us, ' Come to Me, all who labour and are burdened, and I will refresh you '; and again, ' If anyone thirsts, let him come to Me and drink.'

8. My soul hath thirsted for Thee, and my flesh how often ; my habitation, O Lord, is in a desert land, where there is no way and no water. Thou hast given me a parched land, do Thou water it from above ; for my misery, by which I am afflicted in this life, is not small, and wherever I turn myself I find sorrows and labours. I therefore beseech Thee not to be angry with me, for my spirit is troubled in me, and my words are full, not of murmuring, but of sorrow. I have poured forth to Thee my prayer, and I have made known my trouble to Thee. It is often a consolation to the miserable to reveal his trouble to a friend

when the inflamed wound is opened ; it pains less, and is more quickly cured. To Thee, therefore, O Father of mercies, I have made known my state.

CHAPTER XVII

THE CONSOLATION OF THE AFFLICTED AND SORROW-FUL IN TROUBLE

1. *LORD :* What do you wish that I do to thee ? Be more confident, My son. Seeing I have seen the affliction of My people that is in Egypt, and I have come down to deliver them. Be mindful that I am thy Saviour and Redeemer. Be not afflicted, for I who was speaking am present. Why, therefore, are you consumed with grief ? Remember the word which I promised to My disciples : ' I will not leave you orphans, but I will send to you the Spirit of Truth promised by My Father, that He may remain with you for ever.' For it is He who consoles the hearts of the saints in adversity.

2. *Servant :* O Lord, Thou didst say this to Thy Apostles and disciples, and didst fulfil Thy promise to them ; but as I was not there, I do not know how it will be done to me.

Lord : But do you not wish to become My disciple ?

Servant : I do.

3. *Lord :* What I said to them I say to all, for

9

I receive the little and great.   I asked My Father, not only for them, but also for those who would believe in Me by their word.   Everyone who wishes to be a disciple of Christ will be a partaker of all the gifts which I promised to My elect.   I chose and appointed them to go forth, and to bring fruit in patience, and their fruit shall remain to life everlasting.   I say this to you that you may have peace in Me, and that you may keep your soul in patience.   I leave you My peace, I give you My peace ; not as the world gives do I give.   Be patient and willing to receive adversity.

4. Do not fail in tribulation, for tribulation is a consuming fire ; it cleanses from sin, it extinguishes presumption, it banishes dissipation, it introduces a salutary sorrow, it inspires a hatred of worldly things, and it makes us imitators of Christ.   Do you wish to be deprived of these blessings ?

Servant : No, Lord.

Lord : True wisdom affects these blessings in tribulation.   Do not in future seek peace unless in God—the peace and joy of the Holy Ghost, which the world cannot give.

Servant : O peace and joy of my Lord Jesus Christ, who coming from heaven dost in many ways communicate Thyself to the minds of the elect ; O peace and joy in the Holy Ghost, which are not given to the wicked, but to the humble and devout servants of God—oh that Thou wouldst open the heavens and descend to me, and often visit my poor soul, that I could say from experience how benign is the Spirit of Wisdom, how great peace to the lovers of Thy law, and how delicious the sweetness of the Holy Ghost.

5. How willingly I would then despise all perishable and worldly things, and always desire His sweetness ! How patiently I would receive all adversity, and would not feel, by reason of His love, anything to be burdensome ! How gracious, O Lord, is Thy Spirit, who givest this sweetness to Thy children of grace, and with most sweet bread from heaven fillest the hungry souls with interior gifts, and sendest away empty the fastidious rich, who were not worthy of the consolation of the Holy Spirit ! One and the same Spirit does all these things, giving to each one as He wills, helping our infirmity, consoling us in our pilgrimage during our great exile in which we are placed.

CHAPTER XVIII

PATIENCE IS RECOMMENDED FROM THE WORDS AND EXAMPLE OF CHRIST AND OF THE PATRIARCHS

1. WHERE, O good Jesus, is the word of our salvation, which Thou didst speak in the sadness of Thy soul ?—' My soul is sorrowful even unto death.' And immediately after He said to His disciples, ' The hour cometh when the Son of man shall be

delivered into the hands of sinners to be crucified and put to death.' And in another place, 'Father, save Me from this hour.' Therefore Thou camest to this hour, O good Jesus, that Thou wouldst die for the people, and that the whole race should not perish. For unless the grain of wheat, which is Christ the Lord, falling into the earth, died, it alone remained; but if it died, it would bring forth much fruit.

2. O happy and blessed hour, in which man was redeemed from eternal death! O very joyful and grateful sorrow, which took away the lasting grief of our perdition, and restored to mortals all the lost joys of paradise! This was the fruit, O Jesus, of Thy sacred passion, and of Thy many sorrows assumed for us, that Thou wouldst restore lost man to eternal life.

3. Therefore that was not an hour of joy, but of sadness; not of consolation, but of trial; not of peace, but of suffering, as Thou, O Jesus, didst say to the rabble, 'You came to seize me as a robber with swords and sticks.' That was an hour full of storm and clouds, for the Jews cried out in anger, 'Crucify Him! crucify Him! He is guilty of death.' But Jesus was silent; and when He was accused by the chief priests He did not answer.

4. Why do you now complain, my soul? Tell me, where is your patience? You are guilty, and Jesus suffered for you; you have sinned, and He was scourged; you committed enormous crimes, which could not be blotted out unless by the death

of the innocent. What, therefore, will you return to Him for all He has given to you ? or what recompense will you give for your soul ? He gave His life for you; what will you return to Him ? ' I will ' (I say) ' take the chalice of salvation, and call on the name of the Lord.' Very justly, and if you will be grateful, endeavour to drink it.

5. *Lord :* Can you drink this chalice which I drank ?

Servant : And I said, I can do all in Him who helps me. But He, ' Drink all of it ; drink My wine which I have mixed for you '; and again I say to you, ' Unless you eat the flesh of the Son of man and drink His blood, you shall not have life in you.' And do not say in your hearts, This is a hard saying, and who can hear it ?

6. Look on Me, and see that I alone have borne the weight of the day and the heat. And if there were some who bore a heavy burden, yet what is it in comparison to Mine ? I stood fast in the deep mire, and there was no sin in Me ; alone I have trampled the vine-press, and of the people there was not a man with Me. The wicked wrought upon My back, and prolonged their iniquity. See My hands and feet, for I was crucified for you.

7. Put forth your hands and know the place of the nails ; feel my wounds, and see that water and blood flowed from My side ; approach and open your hearts to receive the precious fluid,

and to fill them with the oil of mercy and grace.
Draw forth honey from the rock and oil from the
hard stone.   I have opened the door of My heart ;
enter into it.   I have allowed My side to be pierced
with a lance ; hide yourselves in it.   What more
could I do, and have not done it ?   Answer Me.
Abide in Me, and I in you.   Suffer willingly for
Me, who bore so much for you.   You should not
fear the cross that is before you, for I have made
it light and bearable by My example.

8. Approach Me, all who are in sorrow, who are
interiorly troubled, and who have no consolation.
I am your consoler ; why do you fear in the evil
day ?   I am your protector, your helper in need
and tribulation.   Tell Me, when was I absent from
those hoping in Me ? when was I deaf to those
calling on Me ?

9. What is written in the psalm, and how do
you read it ?—' The Lord is nigh to them that are
of a contrite heart, and He will save the humble
of spirit : the just cried to the Lord, and He heard
them, and delivered them from all their troubles.'
Behold with what words He exhorts you, that you
fail not in tribulation.   You should rather rejoice
that you are afflicted in this world, and look on it
as a proof of love, as a true sign of My elect.

10. Open the book sealed within and without
(the New and Old Testament) ; read and understand that there was never a saint who was not
sorely tried by various temptations and passions,
who did not suffer injuries, and who by sufferings

did not become more acceptable to God and holier before Me.

11. My servants became better by adversity and sufferings, and showed forth the odour of their innocence by patience. Abel was not proved to be good till the malice of Cain tried him ; one is not known to be chaste till he overcomes the risings of the flesh ; the lover of purity is he who, with Joseph, the chaste youth, resisted the temptations of the woman soliciting him.

CHAPTER XIX

PATIENCE IS TO BE PRINCIPALLY EXERCISED IN THE MORTIFICATION OF OUR OWN WILLS

1. HE who strives to go against his own will is proved to be truly obedient ; and this one, as faithful Abraham, will be praised and blessed for the virtue of obedience, and shall be filled with heavenly benediction, because he was obedient to the voice of God rather than the voice of the flesh. And what shall I say of self-will ? It is that which My soul mostly hates. Whatever is not profitable to Me is vitiated by self-will ; it corrupts what is good, both great and small, just as true obedience renders all things perfect.

2. A person may do good from self-will, and it will be of little value ; it may be sometimes even culpable. Omit from obedience a good act, and the omission becomes better. For obedience in-

creases to the contempt of one's self, and draws us to Jesus, the Son of God, and to the example of His obedience. How few do I find who are remarkable for this example of obedience! Each one willingly does what seems to him good, and therefore often falls into mistakes.

3. Know, sons of obedience, that it is never lawful to do wrong, but to sometimes omit a good work, through obedience, conduces to perfection. For as true charity does not seek itself, so true obedience always tends to see good outside itself.

4. You obey Me when you are subject to those over you ; you live to Me when you sacrifice yourself through obedience. I have given you life. I was crucified for you, and you live to Me if you die with Me. Mortify, My sons—mortify your self-wills, your own opinions, your own judgments, and every bad and carnal desire. Kill those enemies, otherwise they shall kill you ; they shall be beams in your eyes, lances in your sides, serpents in your paths, and bears in your way, if you do not kill them. They will not allow you to sleep with a peaceful conscience ; they will take away peace from your heart, because these are they that disturb Israel—that is, the faithful soul desiring to see God. I have admonished you ; see, therefore, that you walk cautiously, for the days are bad, and abstain from all kinds of evil.

CHAPTER XX

PATIENCE IS TAUGHT BY THE EXAMPLE OF THE PROPHETS AND MARTYRS

1. I PROPOSED to you the patriarchs, but if this be little I will now add the prophets, for they experienced many tribulations in this wicked world. The first said: 'I found tribulation and sorrow, and I called on the name of the Lord.' 'Tribulation and anguish found me, but I have not been forgetful of Thy commandments.' 'Many are the trials of the just, but the Lord delivered them from all.'

2. Consider, moreover, the force of the words; for the prophet always finds in himself labour and sorrow, but he obtains help to overcome them when in his distress he cries to the Lord. He said this also: 'When I was in trouble I cried to the Lord, and He heard me.'

3. A second said: 'Therefore do I weep, and tears run down from my eyes, because the Comforter and Converter of my soul is far from me. I am become the scorn of every people; He filled me with sorrow, and inebriated me with bitterness. He broke all my teeth, and fed me with ashes; my soul was rejected, and I forgot all goods, and I said, My end has perished, and my hope from the Lord.' Be attentive to these words, for they are those of lamentation, and Jeremias

the prophet wrote them.　But he also found consolation, for he added : ' The Lord is my part,
for my soul said, Therefore I will expect Him ; the
Lord is good to those who hope in Him, to the
soul seeking Him, because the Lord will not reject
us for ever.'

4. A third said : ' Woe to me, for I am become
as one that gleans in autumn the grapes of the
vintage ; there is no cluster to eat ; my soul desired the first ripe figs.　The holy man is perished
from the earth, and there is none upright among
men.'　But he consoled himself, saying, ' I will
look towards the Lord, and I will wait for God my
Saviour ; my God will hear me when I sit in darkness.　The Lord is my light ; I will bear the
wrath of the Lord, for I have sinned against Him.
He will bring me forth into the light, I shall behold
His justice.'　Behold the testimony of the
prophets, how their hearts were pierced with
sorrow and their spirits were consoled in God.

5. You also know the patience of Job, the great
mirror of patience given for the consolation of all
My servants.　You are not ignorant also of the
many sufferings, persecutions, and temptations of
My saints ; for all those, and especially the holy
martyrs, were proven by great torments, and were
victorious over their persecutors by patience.

6. Now, if you consider well, you shall see that
no one is worthy to be crowned unless he has law-
fully fought, for it is in battle the true soldier is
proven.　If you refuse to bear the assaults of

temptation and the afflictions of tribulation, there will be no victory, and if there be no victory there will be no crown.

7. Therefore the Apostle St. James said, ' Count it all joy, when you shall fall into divers temptations.' And St. Peter said, ' Blessed are you, if you suffer for justice.' And St. Paul said, ' For to you it is given for Christ, not only to believe in Him, but also to suffer for His sake. You also, being admonished by the teaching and example of these, keep patience always in your hearts, and resign yourself to me in all anguish and tribulation. Who can injure you if you be zealous in the acquisition of virtue ? for all your sorrows are numbered, and you shall be crowned for the smallest suffering. Remember that suffering is the life of the saints, by which the kingdom of heaven is reached.'

CHAPTER XXI

PATIENCE IS RECOMMENDED FROM THE CONSIDERATION OF ITS USEFULNESS, OF ITS SHORTNESS, AND OF ITS ETERNAL REWARD

1. Console yourself in becoming by suffering like to Christ your Lord and God, and give thanks if you are able to bear a little for Him. I tell you there is greater merit in suffering than in doing.

2. I seem to have many servants, but they are able to suffer very little ; they are broken down

with a little tribulation, they are irritated by a little contempt, they are scandalized at trifles, they quickly complain of an injury ; when they are rebuked, they think on many excuses.   This is not the right way ; it is very different from My way, and that of all My saints.

3. Some even say they have little peace, and I say they have indeed little peace, because they do not practice patience ; they have not peace, because they follow their own wills ; they are carnal, and live according to men.   Whence come the internal strifes and wars in you but from your own concupiscence ?   You shall not find peace in this life but in your patience.   The more patient you are, the more peace you shall enjoy.

4. My peace I give you, not as the world gives it.   My peace is in much patience, in bearing injuries, and in the contempt of worldly pleasures. For whosoever wishes to be a friend of God should act thus.   I have not come to send peace to the world, but the sword.   Peace shall be on earth to men of goodwill, because there is no peace to the wicked, said the Lord.

5. Have peace with God, and not with the world ; not with your vices and concupiscences, but that peace obtained by bravely fighting against your passions.   This peace is good and holy, and acceptable to God.

6. Remember also in your tribulation that every labour and sorrow shall in a short time be finished, but the reward will be abundant and

eternal in heaven.   Bear also in mind the damnation of many, and how great are their tortures ; if you cannot now suffer a little, how shall you bear the everlasting torments of hell ?

7. Put your finger into a flame of fire : you shall not be able to bear it.   What, then, will it be if your whole body is cast into the furnace of hell ?   Do not, therefore, fear him who kills the flesh, nor angry with him who afflicts the miserable body, but fear Him who, after He has killed, has power to cast body and soul into hell.   I tell you to fear this, to ponder on this, to often think of this, and you shall see that every tribulation is as nothing.

8. Therefore in all adversity of life be comforted by these words : ' Be patient till the coming of the Lord, because the end of all things will soon be at hand.   The whole world and its concupiscence are only passing, for he who loves nothing in the world bears easily adversity.   All its lovers are deceived, confiding in nothing ; but holy men sigh after eternal rewards, and desire to soon leave the world.

9. They do not desire to have anything in it, but lay up for themselves treasures in heaven. They bear many trials, but protect themselves with the arms of patience ; they would often wish to be free from adversity and suffering, but they commend themselves in all things to My hands, saying, ' Father, Thy will be done.' ' Father, not as I will, but as Thou willest.'   All

whatever God willed He did in heaven, and on earth in the sea and in the abyss ; and therefore adversity does not happen to anyone without His permission and ordination.

10. *Servant :* Lord, Thou knowest all things : Thou knowest what is useful for me ; behold, I am Thy servant, do with me according to Thy word. All Thy judgments are true and just ; Thou humblest this one and exaltest that one, for in Thy hands are all the ends of the earth. Thou art just, O Lord, and Thy judgment is right ; Thou art faithful and holy in all Thy works ; in Thy will all things are placed, and there is no one able to resist Thee ; for Thou hast made heaven and earth and sea, and all contained in the universe. Thou art the Lord of all, and I therefore commend myself into Thy hands, because Thou art my Redeemer, my Liberator from my violent enemies, passions and vices, my Helper in tribulations, my Consoler in afflictions which very much oppress me. O Lord, patience is very necessary for me, patience is my defence. I said to patience, Thou art my sister ; to poverty, Thou art my friend ; and to humility, Thou art my mistress and mother. You are all beloved by the Lord and blessed by the words of His mouth. Oh that they were as agreeable and pleasant to me and to all His servants as they are acceptable to Him ! I beseech Thee now and often to continue with us till the end of our lives, for we shall safely reach our Lord if He remain with us Amen.

CHAPTER XXII

DIVINE CONSOLATION IN SUFFERING FOR CHRIST

'You shall have suffering in the world : but have confidence, I have overcome the world.'—JOHN xvi.

1. IT is said in proverbs and by many that to have a companion in suffering is a comfort to the miserable. Who is this companion so kind and good, and who knows how to have compassion on the miserable and afflicted ? This is our Lord Jesus Christ, who suffered and was crucified for us, who calls Himself in the Gospel the Physician and Pastor of souls, the Consoler of the troubled, the poor, the infirm, the fallen, and the wounded ; there is, He says, no need of a physician for the healthy, but for the sick.

2. And in like manner does holy David speak, giving consolation to the sad : ' The Lord is nigh to those who are troubled in heart.' And again in another psalm, speaking of the tempted and troubled, that they should not despair, God speaks in this manner of Himself : ' I am with him in tribulation ; I will deliver him, and I will glorify him.'

3. It is indeed a great consolation to the sad and afflicted in many ways that Christ was tempted, sorrowful, and afflicted in many trials for us. If it were not useful and good for our souls to suffer and to be tried in this world, God

would not permit it to happen, for He is infinitely good and just in all His works. He did not spare His only Son from suffering; and who are we, guilty of many sins, to dare refuse sufferings sent by Him?

4. For it is just that a sinful and useless servant chastised a little should not contradict his Lord, when the Son, beloved in all things, and in no way culpable, is covered with so many wounds. It is also just that a sick person to be cured should for a short time drink a little of the same chalice of which the healthy Physician drank the full cup of its bitterness offered to Him, that He might purge out all the poison of death, and perfectly cure man, wounded in soul and body, and free him from eternal death.

5. The burden of the servant is therefore very much lightened by the consideration of the far heavier burden of his innocent Lord. The grief of the afflicted is very much assuaged if he diligently consider that sufferings patiently borne are a satisfaction for sins and a hope of eternal salvation. For it is honourable and glorious for the poor servant to be clothed in the same garments as his Lord, and to be ennobled with the purple of the King's Son, with which he merits to be introduced to the banquet of the eternal King.

6. The garments of Jesus are humility, poverty in things even necessary, patience in adversity, and perseverance in virtue. He who accepts the

rod of the Lord as a gift shall receive a crown of greater glory in heaven.   Blessed is he who has intelligence of the needy and poor—that is, of Jesus, who became for us poor and distressed— and who follows Him, bearing His cross in daily labours for the salvation of his soul.

CHAPTER XXIII

THE CONSIDERATION OF THE MOST PIOUS MOTHER THE VIRGIN MARY

'Grace is diffused on her lips.'—Ps. xliv.

1. AH, I beseech thee, my Lady, to open thy mouth in the name of Thy Son, who blessed thee with every spiritual grace.

Mary : I am, you say, the Mother of mercy, full of charity and sweetness ; I am the refuge of sinners, the hope and advocate of the guilty ; I am the consoler of the sorrowful, and the special joy of the saints.   Come to me, all who love me, and I will fill you from the abundance of my consolations, for I am clement and merciful to all calling on me.

2. Come to me, you just and sinners ; I will ask the Father for you, I will ask the Son to be propitious to you by the Holy Ghost.   I invite all, I expect all, I desire all to come to me.   I despise no sinner, but I rejoice in great charity even with the angels of God over a sinner doing penance,

10

that the precious Blood of my Son, shed for the world, may not be lost.

3. Therefore approach me, sons of men, and see my zeal for you with God my Son, Jesus Christ. Behold, I will receive His anger, and by fervent prayer I will appease Him whom you know to have offended ; be converted, return, do penance, and I will obtain pardon for you.

4. Behold, I am between heaven and earth, between God and the sinner, and I obtain by my prayers, that the world may not perish. Do not therefore abuse the mercy and forbearance of God, but avoid every offence, lest His anger and unbearable punishment suddenly befall you.

5. I forewarn my sons, and I beseech my beloved to be imitators of my Son and of your Mother. Remember me, who cannot forget you, for I have mercy on all the miserable, and I am the pious advocate of all the faithful.

6. *Disciple :* O most gracious words, full of heavenly sweetness ! O sublime voice, dewing down from heaven, falling softly, consoling sinners and rejoicing the just ! O heavenly music, that sounds sweetly on the despairing conscience ! And whence is it that the Mother of my Lord would speak to me ? Blessed art thou, most holy Mother, and blessed is the word of thy mouth, for honey and milk are under thy tongue, and the sweetness of thy words is greater than all aromatic spices. My soul was softened as thou didst speak, O Mary ; when the voice of thy consolation

sounded in my ears, my soul exulted with joy, my spirit was revived in me, and my whole interior was inundated with new joy.

7. I was sad, but I now rejoice at thy voice, for it is sweet in my ears ; I was oppressed and desolate, but now I am relieved and comforted. Thou hast stretched forth thy hand from on high and touched me, and I have been healed of my infirmity. I could hardly speak, but now is given me even to sing and to joyfully give thanks to thee.

8. It was burdensome to me to live, but now I fear not to die, because I know that thou art my advocate with thy Son. I retain thee as my advocate, and commend myself to thy mercy from this hour, and in every moment, for the future. For from the time thou didst speak to the heart of the desolate orphan I was suddenly changed for the better, and very much strengthened in my interior. For as I lay prostrate in despair, thy consolation came to me, and raised me up with gladness, saying—

9. *Mary :* What is it, my son ? Who are they who wish to injure you ? Do not fear : I will see to you. My son, I live, and Jesus my Son and your Brother lives, who is at the right hand of the Father, the faithful High Priest and Intercessor for your sins. In Him you shall have unbounded hope, because He is the giver of life and destroyer of death. He was born of me in time, He was begotten of the Father from eternity, and was

given for the salvation of the whole world.
Behold, hope and consolation are from Him,
faith and victory by Him. Let Jesus and Mary
be always in your memory, and you shall not fear
the assaults of the enemy.

10. *Disciple :* O happy hour, when thou, O
most pious Virgin Mary, deignest to be present to
my afflicted heart ! Oh that thy visitation to me
would be longer, to hear thy consoling words,
which very much enlighten and strengthen me,
enliven my interior and instruct me. Blessed are
thy breasts, O Divine Mary, which never cease to
give forth the most sweet milk of consolation ;
for on account of the fulness of grace of the
beloved Son Jesus, whom in infancy thou didst
nourish, thou canst not deny that mercy, which
is proper to thee, when thou often bestowest grace
to him who offends in many ways.

11. O Mother of immense piety, of great mercy
and charity ! O incomparable Virgin, beloved
and venerated by all ! O illustrious Mother of the
Son of God, but common Mother of all Christians,
who loves thee with a heartfelt and special devotion ! O Virgin of virgins, queen of the world,
and mistress of angels, draw me after thee, lest,
falling under the load of my sins, I should remain
in that state. Pour forth grace, send down from
heaven the refreshing dew, that I may be able to
truly feel that thou art the Mother of grace and
flowing fountain of mercy.

12. *Mary :* I am the Mother of beautiful love,

of chaste and holy fear, of pious conversation, and of sweet consolation. Therefore, at the hearing of my name rejoice in your heart, reverently bow to me, and willingly salute me ; for by honouring the Mother you honour the Son, who has God for His Father ; for I am Mary, the Mother of Jesus, and this name will remain with me for ever.

13. Who is Jesus ? Christ, the Son of the living God, the Saviour of the world, the King of heaven and earth, the Lord of angels, the Redeemer of the faithful, the Judge of the living and the dead. He is the hope of the pious, the consolation of the devout, the peace of the meek, the riches of the poor, the glory of the humble, the strength of the weak, the way of the erring, the light of the blind, the support of the lame, the unction of the arid, the help of the oppressed, the encourager of the afflicted, and the singular refuge of the good.

14. Bless the Son with the Mother, and you shall be blessed by the Father. You give Him honour and glory as often as you show me reverence. His glory is my joy, His veneration is my praise. Place me and Jesus as a seal upon your heart, as a sign upon your arm. Therefore, standing or sitting, praying or reading, writing or working, let Jesus and Mary be often in your mouth, but always in your heart.

Disciple : Yes. Amen. Let all people and tribes and tongues serve thee ; let all creatures bend before thee. Let the heavens say, Rejoice, O Mary! Let the earth answer, Hail for ever! Let all the saints confess to thy great name, and let all the devout exult before thee and before the Lamb Jesus Christ, thy Son our Lord.

END OF BOOK III

BOOK IV

ON THE VIRTUES OF A TRULY CHRISTIAN MAN

CHAPTER I

ON STABILITY

'Be ye always steadfast in every work of the Lord.'—
1 COR. xv.

1. TELL me, O Christian, what will convenience, or holiness, or whatever you do, profit you, if you fail to reach the kingdom of heaven ? He is blessed who keeps his heart and body from all wandering, and quickly returns to himself with sorrow and asks pardon.

2. Woe to you, who often wander abroad and spend time without profit, and scandalize others. They enjoy quiet peace who willingly remain in solitude, are devoted to God in private, often pray, write good books, attentively read the Holy Scriptures, and lovingly employ themselves in holy meditations. The idle and talkative are deserving of great correction, and should be separated from the community, lest perhaps they injure the simple and weak, disturb and scandalize them with their vain words and perverse conduct.

3. Ye dissolute and jovial, fear the future torments of the fire of purgatory, where you shall suffer very great torments for every vain and foolish word and thought. It is therefore much better to fear now, to be on your guard, to do penance and to weep, than in future to be ever tortured with the wicked, to always burn in hell, from which you cannot by any means be liberated. If you often think on these things, and seriously consider them, you will soon despise all worldly affairs, and have a great fear of all the pleasures of the flesh, that you may escape eternal punishments, and enter after death into the possession of heavenly joys. But woe now, and greater woe in future, to those who think little of Divine judgments, and look on them as trifles, because they have not experienced them in their bodies.

CHAPTER II

A RIGHT INTENTION IS TO BE DIRECTED TO GOD

'My eyes are always to the Lord, for He will free my feet from the snare.'—Ps. xxiv.

1. In every thought, word, and act have always a right and pure intention towards God. He is the cause of all good merits, He is the giver of eternal rewards, He should be the beginning and end of all your works, that you may not lose the fruit of your labours.

2. If you are mindful of the terrible judgments of God you will not indulge in vainglory. Vainglory and the desire of being publicly praised by men is a most poisonous pest. It is the vainest of things, a sign of pride, and contrary to the grace of God.

3. What therefore will you do, in whom will you trust and hope? Not in yourself, not in man, not in anything in the world, but in thy God and Creator alone, who made you, and who keeps you and all created things in His hand and power, and at the same time without burden and without helper. Say therefore and pray with David in the psalm : ' My eyes are always to the Lord, for He will deliver my feet from the snare.' And again : ' O Lord, before Thee is all my desire, and my sigh is not hidden from Thee.'

4. Having therefore put aside the vain reasons and counsels of men in your necessity, rather with prayers and holy desires have confident recourse to the Lord thy God, who will free your feet from the snare, that you may not be drawn from the right way of virtue and true humility, but continue to the end faithful to God.

5. Every good work done for God rejoices the conscience, enlightens the mind, and merits greater grace ; but every evil work saddens the doer, tarnishes his good name, and hinders the influence of Divine consolation.

6. He who does a thing on account of vainglory, and acts and desires to appear before the

world, soon falls into the mire ; for God is displeased with him. Do not therefore rejoice in the happiness of the world, but always keep yourself in the fear of God, and in the knowledge of your own weakness, for your repeated falls and frequent mistakes will teach you to think humbly and vilely of yourself.

7. Be not given to overmuch praise of anyone in this life, for you do not know what will be the future of anyone ; do not rashly judge one who falls, because God can quickly raise up the penitent. Pray for all and commit all to God.

8. Be vile in your own eyes, that you may be great in the sight of God, who regards the humble, and knows the proud from afar, and suddenly casts them down. If you be despised by men, and others are preferred before you, be not oversad ; for it is better and safer to be humbled with the meek and simple than to be cast away by God with the rich and proud.

9. Be on your guard against praise, fear to be magnified, be ashamed to be honoured, flee reputation, seek to lie hid, prefer to serve God, and to be always employed in holy reading and devout prayer. He is not without praise and honour who despises praise and honour for God. He is not without Divine consolation who esteems as nothing all the joys of this world and willingly bears for Christ all things mortifying to himself, and daily sighs to be with Him in heaven.

CHAPTER III

PRUDENT SPEECH AND BROTHERLY COMPASSION

'Doctor, cure thyself.'—LUKE xli.

1. HAVE always this in your mind before you speak to or correct anyone, lest perhaps you be guilty of a greater sin, by indiscreetly or unjustly accusing another. Be just and prudent, select the time and manner of speaking, attend first to the person and temperament of the man, lest perhaps you wound and lose whom you desire to heal and save.

2. A pious and modest word is agreeable to all, a hard and inconsiderate one offends friends. He comforts with holy words the weak in faith, gives the bread of heaven to the languishing, consoles the sad, gives to the thirsty living water ; he appeases the angry with a soft word, and anoints the tongue of the rabid with honey, lest it injure anyone by its dangerous bites.

3. Lips well instructed and discreet are like a solid vessel ornamented with gold, full of ointment, giving forth balm, and worthy of all honour. By your good words and religious morals seculars are edified, the slothful are moved, the negligent are corrected, the dissolute are converted, the ignorant are instructed, and the pious are inflamed. For men are drawn to despise the world and to amend their lives more

by living example than by many words of secular knowledge.

4. Great science and virtue do not consist in the desire of teaching and correcting others, but of governing yourself, of humbly receiving correction, and of fervently amending your lives : this is great wisdom before God and men.

5. Learn to make things that are indifferent good, not to pass judgment on things you do not know ; to avoid what is bad, to bear with the conduct and defects of the imperfect, and to commit to God what you cannot mend.

6. Consider that God has borne with you in many things, and even now daily bears with you, and yet you do not amend, as you have often said and promised ; but He patiently bears with you, and waits for you, that you may do penance, know your weakness, and humbly beg pardon, and that you do not despise or rashly judge anyone.

7. Bear therefore with your brother in few things, as God bears with you in many ; the devout and humble speak few words, that they may not be interiorly distracted by excess of speech. The proud speak harshly, the angry disturb others, and the corrected are troubled.

8. It is the greatest dignity to be humble to all, to consider yourself inferior to others, and to desire willingly to serve all for Christ, who said, ' I am in the midst of you, as one who ministers.' Let the young learn to be silent before they

speak, that they may not be put to shame before the old, for it is safer to be silent than to speak foolishly.

9. It is a great art to know how to be silent when you are corrected; it is great wisdom to speak modestly and, at the proper time, what is just and becoming. The fool knows not how to observe time, manner, or order, and therefore falls into many errors and is justly condemned. The rash youth, hasty to speak, is like a fool and is near a fall.

10. If he who is instructed listens, and he who is corrected is silent and obeys, there will be great hope of proficiency. It is great pride to be steadfast in your own will contrary to God, and to be unwilling to conform to the words and counsels of seniors. But as it is difficult for men to order well their words and actions, sincere Christians should therefore choose and seek to remain in private, to flee the multitude, and to be devoted to prayer.

CHAPTER IV

THE GREAT MERITS OF PATIENCE FOR CHRIST

'In your patience you shall possess your souls.'
LUKE xxi.

1. WHEN anyone speaks harshly to you or unjustly reproaches you, be not angry on a sudden, nor answer roughly; but be silent or speak

humbly, and bear patiently, as did Jesus; for being accused by many, He was silent; and being scourged, He murmured not.

2. But if it be necessary and right to speak, answer kindly and instruct prudently, as Christ, who, being struck with a blow upon the face, answered the servant of the high-priest with gentle and meek words. By acting thus, you will greatly edify others, and free yourself from confusion. In all occasions and in every contradiction be patient and carefully silent about what is said.

3. In all things attend to the profit of your soul and to the great merit of the virtue of patience, which adorns the soul and leads it to victory with the martyrs. Christ taught this, and proved it by His acts during His passion; for when He was accused by the chief priests and rulers of the people He did not answer. What He taught in His instructions He did by His actions. 'Learn of Me, for I am meek and humble of heart, and you shall find rest for your souls.'

4. True rest and secure peace are nowhere found but in God alone, in true humility and benign patience, by which every contradiction is overcome. Let therefore your entire hope be in God, and not in any creature great or small, because without God all things are vain, and with God everything is good.

CHAPTER V

THE REMEMBRANCE OF THE PASSION OF THE LORD IN OPPOSITION TO DISSIPATION

' Blessed are they who mourn, for they shall be comforted.
—MATT. v.

1. By whom ?   Certainly by Christ in the secret of their hearts, and not by the world with vain things.   Light and jocose words and frequent laughter are not becoming the sacred passion or wounds of Christ.

2. Oh that I could bitterly weep for the pardon of all my sins !   How holy the sorrow and how sweet the tears abundantly shed from compassion of the holy wounds of our Lord Jesus Christ !

3. When therefore you are burdened, tempted, and feel languid, immediately grasp the shield of prayer, and seek in the interior of the wounds of Christ a salutary medicine for your vices by earnest prayer and serious meditation on His passion.   Keep the arms of the passion of Jesus Christ beside you as a safeguard by night and by day, lest the devil, the envious enemy, find your mind empty of pious thoughts, and tarnish it with foul images.   Therefore rest here in the peace of Christ, that you may now rise with Him in virtue and grace, and on the last day in eternal glory with His elect.   Amen.

CHAPTER VI

THE INVOCATION OF THE HOLY NAME OF JESUS AND OF THE BLESSED VIRGIN MARY HIS MOTHER

'Direct, O Lord my God, my way in Thy sight.'—Ps. v.

1. THY ways, O Lord Jesus Christ, are pleasant, clean, and safe, in which to justly and perfectly walk ; and all Thy paths are peaceful and holy, to lead all Thy faithful and humble of heart to Thy heavenly kingdom.   Wherever, therefore, you go, walk, stand, or sit, invoke Jesus and Mary, His pious Mother, and willingly read this pious verse as a safeguard in the way : ' Direct, O Lord my God, my way in Thy sight '; and afterwards add this likewise : ' Perfect, O good Jesus, my steps in Thy paths, that they may not be moved ' to see vain things, and to speak what would be foolish and hurtful to my soul.

2. After these, you can also devoutly read this sweet verse in your frequent prayers : ' Jesus and Mary, be always with me in the way, in every place and at every time, lest perhaps I go astray by wrong paths, and may be distracted by many things from within and without. This holy prayer is helpful to console, powerful to assist, prudent to direct in the right path to eternal life, every poor pilgrim and despiser of the world. This holy prayer has with it better companions

and more powerful soldiers than all the kings and princes of the world. This holy prayer draws to itself all the heavenly court, who follow with great reverence the Lord Jesus Christ and the Lady, holy Mary, the Mother of Jesus, worthy of all praise, and honoured by all.

3. He who will have these as companions in his journey through life shall find them powerful advocates at the time of death. Do not forsake them, if you wish to live and always rejoice with Jesus and Mary. He therefore goes well and safely who thinks of Jesus and Mary, who often speaks of them, who blesses them, looks up to them, clings to them, and devoutly honours them.

4. Blessed is he who often invokes Jesus and Mary, who piously salutes and lovingly commemorates them, who exceedingly honours and ardently loves them, and who joyfully celebrates and sings forth their praises. Oh, how sweet is Jesus, and how sweet is Mary, His beloved Mother! Blessed is the pilgrim who in every place and at every time of his exile remembers his heavenly country, where Jesus and Mary rejoice with all the angels and saints in perfect happiness and eternal glory.

5. Blessed is the pilgrim who does not desire an abode in this world, but wishes to be dissolved and to be with Christ in heaven. Blessed are the poor and needy, who daily labour for the bread of heaven, and who cease not to humbly crave before

the throne of God till they receive a crumb of it. Blessed is he who is called to the supper of the Lamb, and receives Him sacramentally, till he reaches the heavenly banquet.

6. For so often as anyone piously communicates, or a priest reverently and devoutly celebrates, so often does he spiritually eat and drink with the blessed Jesus and Mary His blessed Mother. This one is a disciple of Jesus, a companion of the angels, a fellow-citizen of the Apostles, a domestic of God, and a relation of the saints. This one flees the crowd, avoids idle conversations, thinks on the words of Jesus, carefully keeps guard over his heart and all his senses, that he may not offend Jesus and Mary and all the saints.

7. This one shall receive mercy and blessing from the Lord Jesus Christ His Saviour, and as soon as he will cry to Him, in whatever place or trial he may be in, He will hear him from His holy heaven. For when the disciples were passing over the sea, and in fear of being drowned, they called on Jesus, who was present, and He at once said to them : ‘ Why do you fear ? Have confidence : I am here. Fear not.’ For it was the voice of Jesus—a voice anxious to console, powerful to protect, ready to give pleasure, and gracious to bestow eternal life.

CHAPTER VII

ON HUMILITY

'Learn of Me, for I am meek and humble of heart.'—
MATT. xi.

1. O SALUTARY example of humility, who could teach and exemplify such true humility as the God-made man ? And if I had no other example of true humility than Thee, my Lord Jesus, Thou alone wouldst be quite sufficient. If the Son of God, who created all things with His Father, wished to have nothing in the world, what do you always seek and love in it ? Fear what He said : ' You are of the world.'

2. Be converted, ye sons of men, for I am not with you if you be exalted ; if you be proud, you shall fall before your enemies, who will mock you, for bear in mind that I resist the proud. Be humble under My powerful hand, and I will exalt you ; for everyone who humbles himself shall be exalted, and he who exalts himself shall be humbled. How many wished to ascend, and fell as a stone into the abyss ! Pharaoh and his chariots were submerged in the Red Sea. Adam and Eve were driven out of Paradise. Lucifer and his companions were cast from heaven, and in punishment of their pride incurred eternal death.

3. Alas, alas, O Lord ! who will save me from the face of Thy anger ? Thou didst cast them

down whilst they wished to ascend. Babylon
fell—fell, and great was its ruin. But what shall
I do, miserable man ? Whither shall I flee ? I
tremble and fear, for God did not spare either
angels or men guilty of pride. Woe to me if I be
exalted, and woe to me again if I do not humble
myself.

4. O Lord, who watched over me from my
youth, do not abandon me. Let Thy Holy Spirit
lead me in the right way ; enliven me in humility
on account of Thy name. It is humility that will
save my soul and preserve it from eternal loss
If I am humble, I shall be saved. 'Remember
me, O Lord,' said the humble and contrite thief,
'when Thou wilt go into Thy kingdom.' And
Jesus said to him, 'This day you shall be with Me
in Paradise.'

5. 'Adam, where art thou ?' 'O Lord,' he
said, 'I heard Thy voice, and was afraid,
because I was naked.' Miserable man, what
made you naked unless your pride ? If you will
place, O proud man, your abode in the heavens,
I will draw you down, said the Lord. We have
heard of the pride of Moab : he is very proud ;
his pride and arrogance are greater than his
strength. What are you, O proud, but earth and
ashes ? You are earth, and unto earth you shall
return.

CHAPTER VIII

THE CONDUCT AND ACTIONS OF THE TRULY HUMBLE, AND ALSO THE QUALITIES OF THE PROUD

1. IF the humble be rebuked and accused, he makes no excuses and gives no replies, but shows his humility by confessing his fault and promising amendment. Why ? Because he wishes to please God rather than men.   He who fears Divine judgment, at which hidden things shall be made manifest, esteems very little confusion before men. Whoever humbly confesses now his fault shall then receive the pardon of his sins.

2. The humble, whether justly or unjustly reprehended, says, ' I have sinned, I have done evil before Thee.   I am prepared for punishment ; my sorrow is always before me ; I will publish my iniquity, and think of my sin.'   He feels the wound of sin within, and therefore easily bears without whatever is mortifying.   This is indeed a great proof of humility, to confess one's sin when reprehended.

3. Some, on the contrary, act proudly by excusing and defending themselves before others. Their pride suggests to them to say, ' I have not done it ; or, if I have done it, I have done it well ; but if badly, not very badly, and by no means as badly as you say.'   Who is the man who speaks such things of me ?   And he, moreover, some-

times talks in public of his perverse conduct after this manner : ' I was talking in that place, I did such things, I answered so, I said this.'   Oh, what misery and blindness to acknowledge that you have done wrong, and are unwilling to hear from others that you are a sinner !   O sons of men, why do you love vanity, and seek after lies ?

4. A deficiency of grace is caused by the hindrances of pride.   Draw first the beam from your own eye, and then you shall see what I will do to My humble servant.   When have I denied grace to the humble ? and when have I not heard the prayer of the poor ?   Hear the prophet : ' The poor man cried to the Lord, and He heard him, and delivered him from all his tribulations.' ' The Lord regarded the prayer of the humble, and did not despise his prayer.'

5. Many approach Me with a proud heart, and I do not hear them ; they desire devotion, but they are unwilling to suffer confusion with Me ; they desire humility, but they refuse to be despised by men with the humble ; they would like to love virtue without hating vice, and they fail in their desire.   For he who wishes to taste the sweetness of virtue must root from his heart vices and the brambles of his passions.

6. The humble strive to destroy all pride of heart ; they hate all superiority over others, to desire which is great wickedness, for this made the angels devils and men sinners, for everyone who is proud of heart is sinful before God.

7. Woe to you who are great in your own eyes and prudent in your own thoughts. Woe to you who believe that everything that is high is holy, and say to everything sublime, ' It is the honour of God and His glory.' Why do you deceive your hearts ? ' You take too much upon you, ye sons of Levi.' Do not walk in great and wonderful ways above you, but bend your necks, you rebels. If you do it not, I will exalt Myself against you, and I will call on heaven and earth and all the elements to oppose you, and the universe will fight with Me against the foolish and proud.

8. Woe to you who ascend to the side of the north upon the very high mountain, that you may see all the kingdoms of the world and their glory, and say, The tower of Babylon is our hope : there we will sit and rejoice. But it shall not be so, nor shall their words be true. They shall hear for their song weeping. ' The daughter of Babylon is miserable ; blessed is he who will render to her the chastisement which she deserved.' Behold, the hammer and the anvil, the lash and the rod, the gnashing and weeping, shall be upon the arrogant ; depression and fall, ignominy and con-fusion, upon the presumptuous.

9. Do not therefore raise yourself on high, and do not speak wickedly of God, but humble yourself to the lowest in the community in which you live. The foundation of virtue is humility, and other foundation cannot be placed except that which was laid by Christ Jesus. This foundation is placed

in the holy mountain, for the Lord loved the gates of Sion above all the dwellings of Babylon. He who has humility loves and guards it, sleeps and rests in the peace of Christ, as He promised to the humble—' Learn of Me, for I am meek and humble of heart, and you shall find rest for your souls.'

CHAPTER IX

ON THE CLEAR INTELLIGENCE OF THE HOLY SCRIPTURES

'The declaration of Thy words enlightens and gives understanding to little ones.'—PS. cxviii.

1. WHATEVER things are written in the Old or New Testament are written for the instruction of our souls, that we may faithfully serve God by hating sin and loving God, the supreme good, with a pure, whole, and perfect heart, both now and in the future.

2. If you have been unable up to now to understand great things, then learn little things with the little ; as the Lord Jesus said, ' Suffer little ones to come to Me, for of such is the kingdom of heaven.' Do not rashly inquire into those things which are above your intellect, but commit them to the Holy Spirit, and firmly believe, because the Holy Ghost is the teacher of all truth, and He cannot be a witness of falsehood. You should not, on account of application to study, discontinue prayer and Mass ; for often in prayer

and at Mass many secrets are laid open to the devout which are hidden from the proud and curious inquirers. It is very useful to little ones and to the unlearned to explain simple things, but subtle questions are hurtful to them. So long as a man is in this mortal state he can learn more and more, and acquire greater knowledge ; but to the clear intelligence of the angels and to the vision of the saints he cannot reach, till with the assistance of Christ he is in possession of the glory of eternal happiness.

CHAPTER X

IN PRAISE OF THE HOLY ANGELS

' In sight of the angels I will sing to Thee.'—Ps. cxxxvii.

1. O HIGHEST KING, O God worthy of infinite praise, Creator of all things, of angels and men, how long shall I remain on earth, and be removed from Thee and from all Thy holy angels in heaven? Alas, poor and unhappy ! how long shall I eat with men earthly bread, bread of labour and sorrow, and be deprived of the bread of angels, containing the sweetness of every joy ?

2. O Lord, when shall I hear the sound of Thy praise from the mouths of Thy angels in heaven, as St. John the Apostle, banished into exile, heard the voice of a multitude of angels singing together, ' Holy, holy, holy.' Oh that I were one of them,

and had such a voice, how willingly I would praise
Thee with them, sing all the great canticles of
heaven, and magnify Thy holy name for ever !
O Cherubim, O Seraphim, how sweetly, how beautifully, how fervently and excellently, do you sing
the praises of God, without any tediousness,
fatigue, or intermission of your eternal happiness !

3. Therefore all honour and glory is vanity and
smoke to me; everything precious and noble is vile
and deformed—moreover, all things are as nothing
in comparison of eternal life, eternal glory, and
eternal joy in the sight of God and His angels.
But as I am unable to ascend to these sublime
canticles of heaven, and to fully comprehend them,
therefore do I weep and greatly despise myself,
and on my bended knees before God and men
I humbly ask pardon ; for my works are truly
nothing without the grace and mercy of God.

4. Oh the depth of the riches, wisdom, and
knowledge of God, how profound are Thy judgments, and true from the beginning to the end,
upon the good and bad, the grateful and ungrateful, the pious and impious, so that no one can fully
investigate Thy works or justly complain of any
unforeseen event. Therefore may my God be
blessed for ever.

CHAPTER XI

THE PRAYER OF THE DEVOUT LOVER AND PRAISER OF GOD

' Let my prayer, O Lord, ascend as incense in Thy sight.'
—Ps. cxl.

1. I DESIRE, O Lord my God, to devoutly praise, bless, and glorify Thee in every place, and at all times, with all Thy saints and creatures, to always love Thee with a pure heart, and to magnify and ever extol Thy holy name above all things ; for Thou art my God, and I am Thy poor servant. Thou art my light and hope, my God ; Thou art my strength, my patience, my praise and glory, my God ; Thou art my wisdom, my prudence, my beauty and my sweetness, my God ; Thou art my helmet, my armour, my bow and my sword, my God.

2. Thou art my treasure, my gold, my silver, my talent to pay all my debts, my God ; Thou art my house, my fortress, my palace, my God ; Thou art my shield, my standard, my tower of strength, and defender of my life, my God.

3. I find and possess all things in Thee, who art beneficent and merciful ; and whatever I seek or desire outside Thee I feel is valueless to me. Open therefore my heart in Thy holy law, and restore to me the joy of my salvation. Expand my heart to run in Thy way, and confirm me in

Thy words, because there is none to help, none to save and lead me to eternal life, but Thee. Hear me, my God, when I cry to Thee. I commend myself to Thee in all things, and I for ever bless Thee. Amen.

CHAPTER XII

THE UNION OF HEART TO BE MAINTAINED WITH GOD

'My soul, turn to thy rest, for the Lord has done good to thee.'—Ps. cxiv.

1. GOD is indeed thy rest, thy peace, thy life, thy salvation, and thy happiness. Therefore all the good works which you do, see, or hear you should always refer to the praise of God, that you may have peace and a good conscience.

2. Do not trust, confide, or exult in yourself or others, but purely, firmly, and perfectly hope in God, who gives all, and works all in all by His immense goodness and clemency, who will give me such grace that I refer all to the praise and honour of the Lord God; that I may do rightly, as I am bound and able to do; that nothing great or small may draw me from God, or render me careless, or disturb or hinder me in anything. But perhaps it is not possible for me to come to these at present but all is possible to God, who can at once unite Himself in love to the devout soul by His grace.

3. But the perfect and pure love of God can do this in a moment, and as often as He pleases, so that, having forgotten all things, I may be perfectly united to Him alone, and vehemently inflamed and dissolved in the fire of His love. O my God, my love in the place of my pilgrimage, when shall I be entirely united to Thee with all the powers of my soul, graciously infused and given me by Thee ?

4. Let every creature be silent before Thee. Thou alone speak to me, be present with me, and enlighten me, who art all in all, and eternally blessed above all the great luminaries of heaven. Happy the soul that is desolate in the world, but consoled by God ; forgotten by men, but known to the angels ; neglected by the bad, but sought for by the good ; despised by the proud, but loved by the humble ; separated from worldly affairs, but interested in spiritual ones ; scorned by the great, but honoured by the little, as dead exteriorly, but alive interiorly ; afflicted in the flesh but joyful in the spirit ; weak in body, but strong in mind ; deformed in appearance, but beautiful in conscience ; fatigued by labour, but refreshed by prayer ; pressed down with burdens, but raised up with consolations ; tempted in the world by the flesh, but elevated to heaven in spirit and joined with Christ.

5. Happy is he who has Jesus and Mary and all the angels and saints friends in this life, guides in the way, counsellors in doubt, teachers in

study, companions in solitude, intimates in conversation, guardians in dangers, helpers in warfare, defenders against enemies, intercessors for our sins, assistants at death, comforters in our agony, advocates at judgment, patrons before God, and conductors into heaven.

CHAPTER XIII

THE WALKING OF A PURE SOUL WITH GOD

'Walk whilst you have light.'—JOHN xii.

1. HE walks with God in light who desires to have nothing of this world, but has his heart fixed on God in heaven ; for there is the hidden treasure of his soul, the Lord Jesus Christ, in whom all things are contained.

2. He is always miserable and in want, whatever he may have, who has not God for his Friend. He has God who keeps His word and loves Him. He truly keeps the word of God who never says an idle word, who shows by his works what he says in words, who seeks not his own glory, but entirely refers to the glory of God all the good he does or sees in others.

3. He who pleases himself pleases a fool, and displeases God. Therefore in all the good that you say or do study to please God, that you may receive from Him greater graces. Why do you glory in the gifts of Nature, when you are mortal,

and shortly to be the food of worms ? Young man, hear the aged. Withdraw yourself from things which distract you, because you shall not find rest, unless you enter into yourself, seek God, and fervently love Him in preference to every good.

CHAPTER XIV

ON PEACE OF HEART AND REST IN GOD

'His place is made in peace.'—Ps. lxxv.

1. WHO is in good peace ? He who is meek and humble of heart.

2. The better one knows how to humble himself and to suffer for God, the greater is his peace. Every burden is light to him on account of God, whom he has in his heart.

3. Blessed is he who speaks with God in prayer, meditation, singing, and reading, and is silent of what is done in the world.

4. Wherever you are, your thoughts accompany you. Good thoughts give joy, bad ones bring sorrow, anger disturbs, envy blinds, and hatred kills. Pious reading instructs, prayer ascends to heaven, and works fulfil the word. A good word purifies the heart, a vain one defiles it, an idle one scandalizes it, a hard one grieves it, a pious one pacifies it, a moral one edifies it, a learned one strengthens faith, and a heavenly one raises the mind to God.

5. Cleanse, therefore, my heart from all evil, and it will be in peace. There is no true peace unless in God and with the virtuous, who] do everything for God, whom they love. Remain in silence, and put up with a little for God, and He will free you from all burden and unrest.

6. A virtuous life and a good conscience give confidence with God in tribulation and in death; but a bad conscience is always in fear and in trouble. An angry man quickly falls from one evil into a greater; the patient and meek make friends of enemies, and find God always merciful to them, on account of their pity towards the erring.

CHAPTER XV

ON THE RECOLLECTION OF THE HEART WITH GOD

'He, who gathers not with Me, scatters, says our Lord Jesus Christ.'—LUKE xii.

1. WHEN you are very distracted and feel no devotion, on account of the many suggestions of the devil, of the unruly passions of your heart, and of the contradictions of men, causing you trouble, endeavour to recollect yourself in private by the Lord's Prayer and the angelic salutation, by prostrating yourself on the ground before the holy cross, or an image of Blessed Mary, or a picture of a saint, made in honour of God and in memory of the saint. Invoke especially Jesus

and Mary for mercy, and that the grace of Divine consolation may be again given to you, and say with holy David in the psalm, ' O Lord, before Thee is my desire, and my sigh is not hidden from Thee. O Lord, Thou art my hope from my youth, and to Thee I have recourse in my tribulation.'

2. O Lord, teach me to love Thee always, to do Thy will, and to leave my own, because this is pleasing to Thee and useful to me. O Lord, never let it happen to me to think, to desire, or to do what is displeasing to Thee or hurtful to another, as Thou hast commanded me and all who serve Thee. When I do otherwise, correct me in Thy mercy, and do not abandon me in Thy anger ; for Thou art my God, and I am Thy poor, frail servant, entirely in need of Thy grace and mercy in all things. Let Thy holy name be for ever blessed above all. Amen.

CHAPTER XVI

ON COMPANIONSHIP WITH JESUS AND HIS SAINTS

'Seek the Lord, and your soul shall live.'—Ps. lxviii.

1. THE soul cannot have anything better or be happier. He who seeks else shall have nothing in the end. If you wish to have a good companion for your consolation, seek Jesus in the manger with the shepherds, or with the holy wise men in the lap of His Mother, or with Simeon and

Anna in the temple, or with Martha in the village, or with Mary Magdalene at the sepulchre, or with the Apostles in the supper-room, in order to receive the Holy Ghost with great joy.

2. Blessed is he who in these and other holy places devoutly seeks Jesus, not corporally, but in spirit and truth. Blessed is he who in every place and at every time seeks diligently Jesus, and longingly sighs for His clear vision and presence, and daily prepares himself for it. Blessed is he who follows Jesus in His cross and sufferings, for in the end it will be well for him to have Jesus, and he shall not fear any harm.

3. Seek not only Jesus, but also the disciples of Jesus and all the lovers of Jesus, who patiently bore adversities for Jesus. For the love of Jesus and of His friends despises the world, and repels from you every vain and inordinate love. Leave, therefore, friends, acquaintances, and external companions, who may interfere with you in retirement and devotion, and seek for your only solace and companions the Apostles and friends of Jesus, who may speak to you of the kingdom of God and the state of eternal happiness, and how through many tribulations you can be joined with them.

4. Therefore approach all the holy men and women, citizens of the heavenly court, the secret tabernacle and oratory, removed from the noise of the world. Approach the Blessed Virgin Mary, and seek from her consolation for your soul by insisting in prayer.

5. Then approach the Apostles of Christ, seek blessed Peter, and go with him to the Temple to pray, or even ascend with him to the supper-room to receive the Holy Ghost. Seek also Paul in Damascus or Ephesus, and go with him everywhere to preach the Gospel, not in body, but in spirit. Behold how he labours more than all, how often he prays, and how often in prayer and contemplation he is wrapped in ecstasy to heaven. This sublime flight is not given to all, and yet he thinks lowly of himself, saying, ' I do not count myself to have apprehended.' And again, in order to instruct the humble in the life and passion of Christ, he said after other things : ' I do not judge myself to know anything among you but Jesus Christ, and Him crucified.' Follow St. Paul, who will lead you by the right way to Christ, and by the cross to heaven.

6. Go further, and approach the Apostle Andrew, preaching Christ in Achaia, and hear the words of him hanging upon the cross for the name of Christ ; fix them in your mind, and, by the inspiration and help of the Holy Ghost, study to fulfil with joy whatever he said of the sufferings of his Master and in praise of the holy cross. Again, seek St. James the Great, imprisoned and killed by Herod, and drink with him of the chalice of sufferings in this miserable life, by patiently bearing labours for the love of God and salvation of your soul.

7. Then proceed and seek St. John, the beloved Apostle of Christ, exiled for His name,

12—2

and separated from all secular affairs and distractions, who was enlightened by Divine revelation to write in mystic words the Apocalypse, giving the state of the whole Church militant and triumphant, and who, after this, was the last of the Apostles to publish the Holy Gospel of the Divinity of Christ for the instruction and consolation of all the Churches.

8. Seek also, for your consolation, the other holy Apostles, spending themselves in the service of Christ, laying down their lives in defence of His doctrine, and edifying many by word and example. Look at St. James the Less, writing the canonical epistle containing the forms of perfection and Christian life. Seek St. Thomas in India, who reverently touched the wounds of Christ, firmly believed, and with fervent love loudly exclaimed, ' My Lord and my God !' Seek also, with great desire, the holy and learned Apostle and evangelist St. Matthew, who wrote in Hebrew letters the Gospel of Christ, so useful to the whole world, and conducive to the salvation of all nations, peoples, and tongues. In like manner, approach with affection the other holy Apostles and disciples of Jesus Christ, preaching the word of life in many places, teaching people, and labouring till death in the vineyard of God. These are the saints and friends of God, who, by shedding their blood, merited the crown of martyrdom and eternal life. Therefore, willingly read the lives and sufferings of the saints, and be consoled by

their labours and sorrows ; for what you do and suffer for Christ is nothing in comparison to the sufferings of the saints and other servants of God.

CHAPTER XVII

OUR COMPLETE HAPPINESS AND LAST END ARE TO BE PLACED IN GOD ALONE

'I shall be filled when Thy glory shall appear.'—Ps. xvi.

1. O LORD, how can a man come to this glory ? By contempt of himself, and of the world, and by an ardent love of heaven. The souls of the saints rejoicing in the kingdom of heaven, and all the faithful fighting and labouring against the temptations of vices, are witnesses of this. The proud devils, carnal men, loving the world, neglecting God, and placing their end and happiness in the goods, honours, and applause of the world, are far removed from the eternnl enjoyment of this glorious end and perfect good.

2. Who, O God, in order to possess, increase, and preserve these, run here and there, labour, study, watch, never rest, or discontinue their solicitude, till they have acquired some of them ? And when they have acquired them, either directly or indirectly, they are not then content, but desire to ascend higher and to glory over others : they are puffed up, boast of their learning, consider themselves great, and desire to be honoured

by others. And yet all that they seek and desire is vain, slippery, and nothing, dangerous, and in the end lost.

3. You, to whom the world is agreeable and this life pleasant, certainly err and deceive yourselves, because you have nothing certain of all your goods, and every day you draw nearer to death and the future judgment of God. There is nothing in this life so pleasant but has some sorrow joined to it. There is nothing in creatures so precious, good, and desirable that can satisfy and render happy the soul of man, free him from all evil, fill him with every good, and make him always rejoice, but God alone, the great, eternal, and immense good.

4. He is the Creator of all things, visible and invisible, of angels and men, who is before all and above all, God ever blessed in all. For what can be sufficiently said or thought of God by any creature in heaven or on earth? For God exceeds all, before whose eyes all things appear vain and as nothing. Therefore, every soul is foolish, and shall always remain poor and miserable, that seeks and loves outside God whatever would separate the mind from the love and honour of God.

5. Great and wonderful are Thy works, O Lord, and it is impossible for me or any creature to think of or scrutinize one of them. What, therefore, shall I do, who am unable to understand what is above me, to penetrate into heavenly

secrets, and to contemplate the face of God with the angels ? I confess myself unworthy to enjoy these great gifts, and to converse with the saints in heaven. Therefore I will always humble myself before God and all men so long as I live, and I will be vile in my eyes, that God may have mercy on me a sinner now and for ever.

6. I will think of all my years in the bitterness of my soul, during which I deserved anger. I will offer myself to God in sorrow and weeping, whom I have offended in word and deed, by sight, hearing, and by all the other senses which He gave me, to serve Him during my life and with my whole heart. But lest I should despair and be cast down in my miseries, I will remember, O Lord, all Thy gifts and all Thy mercies which have been from the beginning, that I may merit to come to Thee safely, with the assistance of Thy grace. Deliver me from all evils suddenly coming upon me, and which often withdraw my heart from meditating on heavenly things. Be present to me, O good God, and place me near Thee, that I may not begin to wander and stray away from the supreme good which Thou art, O Lord. For in Thee is all my good ; give me Thyself, and it is sufficient for my soul, O Lord God of my salvation. Amen.

CHAPTER XVIII

THE APPROACH TO THE HOLY OF HOLIES JESUS CHRIST, THE KING OF ANGELS

' Thou art my King and my God.'—Ps. xliii.

1. ARISE, my soul, come and enter into the place of the wonderful tabernacle, even into the house of God ; for it is becoming that, putting aside all things, you should now with humble reverence proceed to salute the Lord Jesus Christ your Saviour, who is head of every principality and power, the Joy and Crown of all the saints, the firm hope and certain expectation of all the entire faithful.

2. He created and redeemed you, He laboured for you, fought for you and conquered for you ; He is your Advocate and the propitiation for your sins ; He is your Consoler, Provider, and Director ; He is your only and dearly beloved, who feeds among lilies, and delights to remain in your bosom.

3. Who ever did you so much good, who ever loved you with such charity ? Approach Him, and give yourself to Him ; open to Him your heart, and lay before Him whatever you have hidden up to the present. No one will better point out to you or reveal what counsel you should take or what hope you should entertain in human affairs, which circumstances so often change.

4. Let your purposes and desires be with Him,

let your counsels continue with Him ; for the hope
of men is vain, but in Him is stability of peace.
Through Him you have access to the Father, by
Him every grace is given and more abundant
strength imparted.

5. Whether you are sad or whether you rejoice,
have always recourse to Him ; He is the Mirror of
your life, the rule of justice, the unfailing Light of
your soul, the lover of purity, and the Joy of your
conscience.   You can easily despise every pleasure
for Him, you can bear every bitter and mortifying
thing for Him, and contradictions will be pleasing
on account of Him.

6. Finally, from Him, by Him, and in Him
are all things.   Every intention, action, speech,
reading, prayer, meditation, and speculation
should be principally directed to Him.   By Him
salvation is given to you, and eternal life prepared
for you.   On account of Him, you should not fear
to die or refuse to live, because you should have
confidence in His fidelity, and you should not prefer anything to His honour and love.   Therefore
now approach your Redeemer and give Him
thanks.

7. O most sweet and amiable Jesus, may Thou
be most devotedly saluted, most highly praised,
and now and for eternity blessed above by every
creature.   O most excellent Jesus, what honour
can I ever return Thee, or what thanks can I ever
render Thee, who hast shown me infinite mercies ?
And if I could find anything that I could give

Thee, is it not already Thy gift before I give it ?
What, therefore, shall I return to Thee ?   I have
little or nothing, and how can I give Thee from my
nothingness ?   Receive, therefore, the sacrifice
of my poverty, humility, and nothingness, and
whatever Thou hast given me, let it all be ascribed
to Thee.

8. Let all the choirs of angels, always assisting
Thee, pour forth their immense praises for me,
and let all the spirits of the just repeat the same
with great joy.   But yet, what shall I do in
memory and praise of Thy most holy name ?   I
should do many things—I am bound and obliged
to do many things—but I am hardly sufficient for
the smallest.

9. I will, however, read of Thee, my most sweet
Jesus ; I will write of Thee, I will sing of Thee, I
will think of Thee, I will speak of Thee, I will
work for Thee, I will suffer for Thee, I will exult
in Thee, I will praise Thee, I will magnify Thee,
I will glorify Thee.   I will justly adore Thee,
because Thou art my God, in whom I believe,
whom I love, whom I desire, and whom I seek.
Make with me a sign in Thy goodness, that my
eyes may see Thy beautiful countenance in heaven.
At Thy feet I humbly prostrate myself, fervently
imploring with tears Thy clemency, that Thou
mayest deign to be merciful to me.

10. Write my name in the book of life, and never
let that be blotted out which Thy holy hand has
written.   I, unhappy, very unlike the saints in

merits, confiding in Thy infinite merits, implore that I may deserve to be numbered at least among the lowest and least members of Thy elect.

11. I know that such has been my life and conversation that I dare not presume anything of myself, but my whole hope and consolation consist and rest in the price of Thy precious blood, in which I entirely confide, and desire to place all I have done, all I have sinned, all I have merited, and all I have omitted. Behold, therefore, O most clement Jesus, my littleness and my indigence ; look to the affection of my heart, which I bear and have for Thee ; not that I am worthy, but because Thou art kind, and dost not refuse to be approached and loved by the unworthy.

12. My iniquity frightens me, but again Thy great goodness and humility draw and entice me to Thee ; for Thou didst in true charity consent to become not only man, but to suffer, to die, and to be buried for sinful man. Therefore I fly to Thee, for I find nothing good in myself ; supply to me what my strength is unable to do.

13. Thou gavest me the desire to salute, to praise, and to bless Thee, because Thou art my hope and portion in the land of the living. The desire of my soul is to be with Thee in the kingdom of heaven, but as my time is not yet come, I will expect Thee to the end. In the meantime let this be my consolation in the place of my pilgrimage, that I am mindful of Thy name and of Thy exceeding great charity, and that I have

Thee present in faith and in the sacraments of the Church.

14. It would indeed be intolerable for me to live in this world, unless I have hope in Thee, O Lord. For I do not wish to rejoice with the world, and as I could not be without consolation and joy, I have resolved to place my joy in Thee. I should often very much go astray and greatly wander in my thoughts, unless I kept Thee in my memory and imagination. And as I cannot comprehend the height of Thy Divinity, and am not sufficient to understand spiritual truths, it is safer for me to turn to the words and acts of Thy sacred humanity, because by thinking of them I do not entirely depart from Thy Divinity.

15. I give Thee thanks, O good, sweet, and blessed Jesus, because Thou didst deign to become my Brother and my flesh and bone. Thanks be to holy Mary, my Mother, from whose virginal flesh Thou didst assume the sacred members of Thy body, and by means of a rational soul Thou didst perfectly unite it to Thy Divinity, so that she is truly and worthily called, not only the Mother of man, but also of God.

CHAPTER XIX

THE APPROACH TO SALUTE THE GLORIOUS VIRGIN

'The queen sat at his right hand in a robe of gold.'—
Ps. xliv.

1. THOUGH I am without merit and conscious of many sins, yet, O Lord, I have very great confidence in Thy passion, and in the merits of the ever-blessed Virgin Mary Thy Mother, of whom I now wish to speak a little, which, I trust, will be pleasing to Thee. For who am I that I would dare to approach nearer, unless I had first obtained permission. I know my unworthiness should not appear in presence of the very great reverence of her whom the angels venerate with great wonder, saying, ' Who is this who comes forth from the desert of the world, abounding in the delights of Paradise ?'

2. Therefore, O most sweet Mary, it is not becoming me to consider thy glory, honour, beauty, and magnificence ; for I am earth and ashes— more, I am viler than earth and ashes, because I am a sinner, and inclined to every evil. But thou art made higher than heaven, having the earth under thy feet, and on account of thy Son art esteemed worthy of all honour and reverence.

3. But thy ineffable piety, which exceeds all conception, often draws and wins my affection for thee, for thou art indeed the solace of the deso-

late, and art accustomed to willingly help miserable sinners.   I know that I need all the consolations and comforts, and especially the grace of thy Son, for I am by no means sufficient to help myself.

4. For thou, O most pious Mother, if thou deignest to attend to my poverty, thou canst assist me by many aids, and comfort me by thy great consolation in the troubles of the world. When, therefore, I shall be surrounded by any trial or temptation, I will quickly have recourse to thee, for thou art more inclined to mercy, because thou art full of mercy and grace.

5. For if it be sometimes agreeable to consider seriously thy very great glory, and to salute thee worthily from the heart, it is necessary to proceed with very great purity of mind, and to continue it, under the guidance of supernatural light ; for he shall not receive glory, but great confusion, who irreverently presumes to approach thee.   It is therefore necessary for one approaching thee to proceed with great reverence and humility, to which should be joined a firm hope of being admitted by reason of thy great clemency.

6. I therefore approach thee humbly and reverently, devoutly and confidently, having in my mouth the salutation of Gabriel, to be piously addressed to thee, which I joyfully present to thee, with head inclined on account of thy great reverence, and with outstretched hands on account

of the great feeling of devotion, and I ask and pray that this salutation be said for me hundreds and thousands of times, and more, by all the heavenly spirits; for I am entirely ignorant of a more worthy or sweeter salutation to offer at present. Let the pious lover of thy holy name now listen. Heaven rejoices and all the earth is astonished when I say, Hail, Mary! Satan flees and hell trembles when I say, Hail, Mary!

7. The world becomes vile, the flesh powerless, when I say, Hail, Mary! Sorrow departs and new joy comes when I say, Hail, Mary! Torpor disappears, the heart is softened with love, when I say, Hail, Mary! Devotion is increased, compunction is aroused, hope becomes stronger and consolation greater, when I say, Hail, Mary! The mind is refreshed, the wearied affections are comforted, when I say, Hail, Mary!

8. Indeed, so great is the sweetness of this blessed salutation that it cannot be explained by human words, for its meaning is always higher and more profound than any creature is able to fathom. Therefore I again humbly bend my knees before thee, O most holy Virgin, and say, Hail, Mary, full of grace!

9. Receive, O Holy Mary, my most clement Lady, this very devout salutation, and receive me with it, that I may have something to please thee greatly, to give me confidence in thee, to always excite me to greater love for thee, and to keep me in constant devotion to thy most vener-

able name.   Oh that I could offer this most sweet salutation of Gabriel as a holy and pure offering of prayer for all my sins, by which I have displeased thy Son and merited anger, and by which, too, I have often dishonoured and offended the whole court of heaven, that it would be an expiation of all my offences.

10. Oh that also, as I am very frail and unsteady in my life, all the blessed spirits and souls of the just would, with the purest devotion and most fervent supplication, say to thee, most blessed Virgin Mary, and a hundred times repeat in thy honour, this most exalted salutation for all my excesses and negligences, and also for all my vain, unbecoming, and perverse thoughts.   And as by this salutation the Father, Son, and Holy Ghost decreed for the first time to salute thee by the angel, I, who have no goodness or worthy offering, may find in it an acceptable one unto an odour of sweetness.   But even now, prostrate in thy presence, and drawn by sincere devotion, I represent to thee the joy of this salutation, when the archangel Gabriel, sent by God, entered thy private apartment, and reverently on bended knees honoured thy virginal face with a new salutation, never before heard, and said, ' Hail, full of grace, the Lord is with thee.'   I wish to repeat in full, after the manner of the faithful, and with a golden tongue I desire from the bottom of my heart that all creatures would say together with me, ' Hail, full of grace, the Lord is with thee ; blessed

art thou among women, and blessed is the fruit of thy womb, Jesus Christ.' Amen.

11. This is the angelical salutation formed by the inspiration of the Holy Ghost, and becoming thy very great dignity and sanctity. This prayer is small in words, but great in mysteries ; short in discourse, but extensive in virtue ; sweeter than honey, and more precious than gold ; to be constantly pondered on in the heart, and to be often read and repeated by pure lips. Though it is contained in few words, it diffuses widely the torrent of heavenly sweetness.

12. But woe to the fastidious and indevout, and to those who pray with distractions, ponder not on the golden words, taste not their sweetness, and say the Hail, Mary ! without attention and reverence. O most sweet Virgin, preserve me from so great negligence and sloth, and pardon me for my past faults ; for the future I will be more devout, more fervent, and more attentive in saying the Hail, Mary ! in what place soever I may be.

13. And now, after these, what shall I ask of thee, my most dear Lady ? What is better, or what more useful or more necessary for me, an unworthy sinner, than to find favour before thee and thy most beloved Son ? I therefore ask the grace of God by the advocacy and intercession of thee, who, in the angel's words, was found full of grace before God. There is no petition dearer, as there is nothing I so much need, as the grace of God.

14. The grace of God is sufficient for me without all other things; for what is my every endeavour without it? What is impossible with grace assisting and helping me? I have many and divers infirmities of soul, but Divine grace is a most efficacious remedy against all passions, and if it comes opportunely, it cures all. I have also a great want of spiritual wisdom and knowledge, but the greatest instructor and teacher of heavenly discipline is Divine grace, which is sufficient to at once instruct me in all that is necessary. But this grace dissuades me from asking anything more than is necessary, or to desire to know anything beyond what is lawful; and it, moreover, admonishes and teaches me to be humble, and to be contented with it. Therefore, O most clement Virgin, obtain for me this grace, which is so noble and precious that I do not really desire anything but it.

CHAPTER XX

THAT THANKS ARE TO BE GIVEN FOR ALL BENEFITS

'Let the name of the Lord be blessed for ever.'—Ps. lxxi.

1. O LORD GOD, whatever I do, read, or write, whatever I think, speak, or understand, let it be done for Thee. May my every work be begun by Thee and for Thee, and finished in Thee. That

which Thou hast given receive again, and whence
the rivers flow let them return to the same place.
Things are never better with me, and never more
agreeable, than when I sincerely return to Thee
whatever is rightly thought or done by me.

2. I desire to return thanks, and now indeed
do so, when I give all to Thee, and retain nothing
for myself, of all the benefits given by Thee, and
received by me. For what, I say, can I, a bad
and slothful servant, return ? My service is
nothing, even though I do all that Thou hast commanded. Therefore I am reduced to nothing
and in truth humbled. It is good that Thou hast
humbled me, that Thou alone mayest be justified,
Thou alone praised, and that I, vile dust, should
not glory in myself.

3. Nevertheless, I will not desist, but I will
continue to praise Thee with my heart and mouth ;
for though I am unable to worthily do it, yet it
would be unbecoming to be entirely silent, and
not to know that Thou, my God, art my praise,
and to Thee is my rejoicing for ever. He who
feels a little for Thy glory, and what it is to glory
in Thee, esteems very little whatever external
glory may flatter him ; and he who tastes a little
of Thy sweetness considers better all worldly
pleasure.

4. Oh, how much he who has a spark of Thy
charity is on fire ! for he would most willingly
despise all things to be possessed of Thy love,
and whatever he could do or suffer for it would be

light and sweet to him, and he would exult and fervently follow Thee in remembrance of Thy gifts. He would seek nothing dearer, possess nothing happier, follow nothing more earnestly, than what would be agreeable to Thee. The lover feels no weight, for love carries all burdens, and they therefore who complain of burdens testify that they are deficient in love.

5. To serve Thee from love is most pleasant, and gives comfort in labours. Love has no regard to its own convenience, and is not ashamed to suffer, but it seeks in all things Thy good pleasure. How sweet is Thy love, O Christ ! How beautifully it sounds ! how pleasantly it enters into me ! how strongly it holds and binds me ! Oh that it may keep me in Thy continual service, wholly occupy me, entirely master me, and make me one with Thee !

6. Then, indeed, I am perfectly free when I am captured by Thy love, stripped and deprived of all self-love. I am Thy servant, O Lord—Thy servant, I say, because Thou hast redeemed me : willingly I am Thine, and it pleases me to be Thine, for I do not wish to belong to myself ; help me to be freed from all self-love.

7. Enkindle, stir up, and set on fire the little spark, and it will inflame my heart, make it pure, bright and beautiful ; for Thy love banishes all vices, and consumes all sin. Keep me in the bonds of love, which will secure my service ; I know my service will not be any advantage to

Thee, but it will be useful to me to do what I know will be agreeable to Thee. I will indeed act, and not be silent ; I will speak, and not hide Thy works.

8. When shall I be able to thank Thee sufficiently for all the benefits Thou hast conferred on me, who am unworthy of them ? Thou hast, O Lord, done great mercy to Thy servant, and I should blush for not having returned thanks, as Thou hast worthily deserved. Therefore do I feel pain and sorrow because I am unable to make any return for Thy benefits so many and so great. Would that I could even once worthily and sufficiently thank Thee for them.

9. But what can come from him in whom there is nothing ? He is an empty vessel, and has nothing to give. What, therefore, shall I do ? It is necessary to give me something, that I may not appear empty before Thee ; for every ungrateful one is displeasing to Thee. Oh if I had anything in the whole world to give Thee, and to appear grateful in Thy eyes! What dost Thou wish to have, dear Lord ? Thou dost not stand in need of my goods. Why, therefore, dost thou require a gift from me ? No one is richer than Thou, and yet Thou requirest gifts from me.

10. I wish, Thou sayest, to have all ; this is necessary for you, if you wish to merit My grace. I will give grace, and you shall return the gift, and thus we shall have together mutual charity. Give yourself to Me, and you give all. O Jesus,

the Source of all good, the Fountain of life, of grace, of sweetness, and of eternal wisdom, pour now into my heart the gift of Thy heavenly grace, and teach me to always render Thee thanks, and to give myself to Thee before all things, for this is the most precious gift I can make Thee.

11. I know this, and consent to it; receive me. Behold, I am all Thine, and all I have is Thine. There is one thing which I cannot offer Thee. What is it? My sins, which are my own, and therefore not to be offered to Thee. Sins are mine, and many reprehensible defects, to me alone attributable; but to Thee glory and thanks for all Thy benefits.

12. But to enumerate Thy benefits, I will select a few from the many, and those which are more apparent and more powerful to move me; for neither time allows, nor is my mind able to consider all. For their number exceeds measure, their greatness cannot be conceived, and their worth is beyond all price. They cannot be bought, for they are gratuitously given, and therefore gratitude alone is required for them; otherwise they shall all be taken from the ungrateful.

13. I therefore in the first place give thanks to Thee, my Lord God, Creator of all things, that Thou hast deigned to create me a rational being, and to place me over the works of Thy hands; and as to my soul, Thou didst make it to Thy image and likeness. This is the first great benefit given me by Thy generous bounty; for I did not

create myself, but Thou didst make me, bringing me into the world by parents, whom Thou didst make Thy instruments in this matter. And behold, I am greater than other creatures, superior to all animals and birds of the air, because I am made to the image of God, capable of eternal wisdom, and naturally a participator of uncreated light and unchangeable truth.

14. I render to Thee perpetual thanks for all that I am, that I live and understand ; I desire and ask that all creatures in heaven and on earth may praise together Thy admirable name and for ever exalt it. I bless Thee, Father, and Lord of heaven and earth, who created all things from nothing by Thy only Son in the Holy Ghost.

15. Thou created all things of Thy pure and free liberty, and not from any necessity, that Thou mightest manifest Thy power to the sons of men. Thou didst perfectly arrange this visible world by Thy invisible wisdom, co-eternal with Thee. Let all Thy creatures created for the use of the human race bless Thee and be subject to Thee in all things ; for at Thy bidding the heaven gives rain at the proper times, and the earth brings forth many fruits.

16. The sun and moon clearly shine upon the earth, the stars at night keep their courses in order, fountains shoot forth their water, rivers flow, and fishes of divers kinds swim in the sea ; the birds of the air fly and sing, goats, asses, and deer bound in the mountains, sheep and cattle

rejoice in good pasture, and various animals roam through the forests. Pastures are green, fields abound with corn, all the trees of the forest put forth their branches and fruits. These are Thy works, O Lord, who alone does wonderful things.

17. The second benefit which presents itself to me is the mystery of the Incarnation, the work of redemption, the price of our salvation, the fruit, indeed, of Thy Passion and Death. O great work of piety, work of the most excellent charity, of the most profound humility, and of the most singular patience ! Man did not merit it, and none of the angels could do it. The prophets wondered at it, the Apostles saw it and taught it, all the faithful received it, and the elect especially loved it and availed themselves of it.

18. This benefit well considered excites desires, inflames hearts, nourishes devotion, enlightens the mind, purifies the affection, draws us to heaven, withdraws us from the world, leads to Christ, and unites the soul with Him. This benefit is far greater than the former, though it is the one Jesus Christ our Lord God who made and gave both. For it profits me nothing to be born into the world, if He had not redeemed me with His precious blood. Therefore grace came to me, Divine mercy increased, and there was made for me a plentiful redemption, for fallen nature could not be repaired without the help of the Creator.

19. O Father of mercies and God of all Consolation, that Thou mightest redeem a guilty servant, Thou didst deliver Thy own Son. Oh the wonderful greatness of Thy pity towards us, which neither the human mind nor angelic reason is able to explain ! O Jesus, the Source of goodness and pity, the Splendour of eternal light, the Mirror of God's majesty, without spot, set my heart on fire with the thought of this ineffable benefit. How many benefits hast Thou bestowed upon us in Thy humanity ! Thou madest Thyself our Brother and our flesh, that we might be called the sons of God, and by Thee have access to the Father. Blessed is he who merits to receive by grace what the wise of the world were not able to know by nature.

20. O Jesus, the wisdom of the Father, enable me to understand by the light of faith this great and admirable mystery of Thy incarnation ; for in it the sweetness of our entire salvation is hidden, the greatest charity abounds, and the fulness of Thy unsearchable wisdom shines forth. May Thy servant become better by increase in virtue, by doing good works, by being more and more instructed in the knowledge of Thy sacred passion, and wholly drawn to Thyself in this wonderful mystery of Thy incarnation. It is indeed a profound abyss, an exhibition of the greatest charity and condescension, a certain Divine ocean, which cannot be passed, and in which we spiritual fishes, little and great, whom

Thou hast enclosed in the net of faith, swim to and fro.

21. Let, then, so great charity and sweetness, so great humility and meekness, be in my memory; let something of the mystery of the Incarnation and Passion enter into and be continued in every oblation of prayer and exercise of meditation, as the brightest incense and sweetest balsam to be offered in an odour of sweetness to God the Father.

22. Let them now, who are redeemed by the Lord, whom He redeemed from the hand of the enemy, sing forth a canticle of Divine praise, and let them finish with a hymn of mental jubilation. And all the angels standing around the throne fell upon their faces, and adored the Lamb of God, who took away the sins of the world, saying : Praise and honour are due to Thee, O Lord, benediction and splendour, thanksgiving and the voice of praise, strength and power, majesty and wisdom to Thee, Lord, our God Jesus Christ, for all ages. Amen.

23. The third benefit, which is not inferior to the former, is the grace of justification, by which Thou didst mercifully draw me to conversion and amendment of life, giving me sorrow for sins, hope of pardon, purpose of living well, and of serving Thee for ever. The blessed Paul, clearly considering this, exhorted his disciples that they should not be ungrateful for so great a benefit, but mindful of this heavenly vocation. ' See,

brethren,' he said, ' your vocation, that not many wise, not many powerful, but that God chose those who were infirm in the world.'

24. I will consider these things with myself, who am contemptible and useless in the world, and rescued from its shipwreck by Thy holy vocation, and merited to be called to serve Thee, and to be joined to Thy society. And lest I should again turn back, I voluntarily bound myself by vow, which I ascribe, not, indeed, to my deserts, but to Thy providence, for which I greatly praise and bless Thee, because Thou hast deigned to call me by grace, giving me a good will, and casting from me a load of sin.

25. And, besides, Thou hast subjected me to Thy sweet yoke, making my mind gentle by its union with the Holy Ghost, whom the world neither knows, nor sees, nor relishes. Guard this will, O merciful God ; moreover, increase the gift of grace while I am in the world.

I know that this vocation is a great benefit, which is not given to all, but to those for whom it is prepared by the Father ; for it is not to those who will to run, but to the merciful God ; that every mouth speaking vain things may be closed, that the whole man may be subject to Thee, that all flesh may glory in Thy sight, and that no one may attribute to himself anything of his own merits and good works.

26. For if Thou didst wish to treat me according to justice, I should have been sent with those who

are in hell ; but Thy clemency, O Lord spared me, and gave me a place of indulgence, that I should not become a son of eternal perdition. I am therefore bound to render to Thee great thanks for so magnificent a benefit ; and oh that I may respond to it with grateful words and becoming works all the days of my life ! Never let my heart be turned away from Thy love, and let my soul and body always increase and persevere in Thy most holy service, and may I be mindful of Thee so long as life is in me and exercises my reason. Let all Thy servants from the beginning of the world, enlightened and called by Thy grace, and also all faithful Christians and every people, tribe, tongue, and nation, who live at the present time, who were before us, and who shall come after us, unite in celebrating and praising Thy most sweet and glorious name, which is blessed above every name.

And that a most worthy tribute be rendered to Thee, O God, may the Most Holy Trinity, together with the angels and saints, deign to praise Himself now and for ever. Amen.

THE END

R. AND T. WASHBOURNE, 4 PATERNOSTER ROW, LONDON

Other Books by St Athanasius Press

Religious Orders of Women in the U.S.
by Elinor Tong Dehey. Hardcover.
Unedited Reprint of the 1930 Revised Edition. 908 Pages.
Catholic. Retail $59.99

Terra Incognita or Convents of the United Kingdom
by John Nicholas Murphy. 757 pages. Unedited Reprint
of 1873 book. Catholic. Retail $59.99

A Textual Concordance to the Holy Scriptures
Douay Rheims Version by Thomas David Williams
HardCover. Unedited Reprint of the 1908 Original.
848 Pages. Catholic. Retail $49.99

VESTIARIVM CHRISTIANVM: The Dress of Holy Ministry
in the Church-Christian Vestments. Unedited Reprint of the
1868 Original. 406 Pages, 62+ pages of Illustrations.
Hardcover. Anglican. Retail $49.99

Church Ornaments of our Manufacture. 1910 Benziger
Bros Catalog. Softcover. Unedited Reprint of Benziger's
1910 catalog. Fully Illustrated. Catholic. Retail $24.99

Vera Sapentia Or True Wisdom by Thomas A Kempis.
Softcover. Unedited Reprint of 1904 book. Catholic
Retail $19.99

For Ordering info, please email wallmell@aol.com
or call 1-800-230-1025
Or Write: St Athanasius Press/St Joan of Arc Books
133 Slazing Rd
Potosi, WI 53820

Bookstore inquiries are welcome!

Printed in the United States
50045LVS00001B/175-192